Christmas Patchwork Projects

Linda Seward

Sterling Publishing Co., Inc.   New York

EDITED by VILMA LIACOURAS CHANTILES

Library of Congress Cataloging-in-Publication Data

Seward, Linda.
    Christmas patchwork projects.

    Includes index.
    1. Christmas decorations.   2. Patchwork.   3. House
furnishings.   I. Title.
TT900.C4S48   1986   746.46   86-5738
ISBN 0-8069-6366-2
ISBN 0-8069-6367-0 (lib. bdg.)
ISBN 0-8069-6364-6 (pbk.)

Copyright © 1986 by Linda Seward
Published by Sterling Publishing Co., Inc.
Two Park Avenue, New York, N.Y. 10016
Distributed in Canada by Oak Tree Press Ltd.
℅ Canadian Manda Group, P.O. Box 920, Station U
Toronto, Ontario, Canada M8Z 5P9
Distributed in the United Kingdom by Blandford Press
Link House, West Street, Poole, Dorset BH15 1LL, England
Distributed in Australia by Capricorn Ltd.
P.O. Box 665, Lane Cove, NSW 2066
Manufactured in the United States of America

For my sister, Danae

ACKNOWLEDGMENTS

I would like to thank the people who helped in the preparation of this book:

Charles G. Nurnberg, for his support and enthusiasm.

Vilma Chantiles, for making sense out of a patchwork of a manuscript.

Dr. and Mrs. E. C. Seward, for allowing me to rearrange their house during several photography sessions.

My mother, Evelyn Macho, for finding Christmas fabrics in July.

My husband, Robert, for believing in me.

Contents

Block Designs: 12 Inches Square   43

Projects Based on 12-Inch-Square Blocks   116–141

Introduction

Christmas is a time when people feel good about each other, when the family comes home, a time to give thanks. If you feel nostalgic and happy and full of love at Christmastime, this book is for you. On these pages, you'll find fresh new ideas for patchwork presents and decorations for you, your family, and friends to enjoy during the holiday season. And because Christmas items are only used once a year, they will last for many holidays—probably a lifetime!

This book is for people who look forward to Christmas as the highlight of the year, and who enjoy all the hectic preparations that precede December 25. Traditions vary from one household to another, but you'll recognize at least some of these December activities: Cakes and cookies are baked; presents are made or bought and wrapped with special paper, ribbons and bows; Christmas records are brought out from the back of the cabinet and dusted off for another season; the house, inside and out, is decorated with wreaths, lights, candles, and stars; the Christmas manger is carefully unpacked and displayed in a place of honor; presents for faraway relatives and friends are packed and mailed; Christmas cards are written and mailed (always late!); and at last, a Christmas tree is selected and brought home to be decorated with ornaments, lights, and tinsel. Then come the parties and carol singing and church services, culminating in midnight mass on Christmas Eve. Then, of course, there are holiday gifts. . . .

Christmas Patchwork Projects will be an important addition to every quilter's library. It contains a splendid collection of patchwork projects to entice and intrigue both beginning and experienced quilters. All projects and designs have been graded by their technical level of expertise, making it simple for a quilter to select a suitable project. It is a real workbook, too; the reader is encouraged to come up with original ideas and creations, using the book as a guide.

HOW TO USE THIS BOOK

This book is arranged simply for easy use, beginning with Making Patchwork Projects: Techniques, a chapter of instructions on how to piece the patchwork and to quilt. I refer to these vital techniques throughout the book. By familiarizing yourself very carefully with this chapter, it will be easy for you to look back and find the technique under discussion. For example, whenever you are required to add a binding, I will refer you to Binding a Project; look up the page number in the Index, if necessary. For quilting techniques, you'll be advised to see How to Quilt; for intricate sewing, I'll suggest you read How to Inset or Sewing Curves.

Three different chapters follow the instructions. Quick Holiday Gifts & Decorations offers many designs that require specific templates and instructions. Most of these individual projects are quite small and very quick to make. There are many variations on each theme, but the templates and instructions are not interchangeable.

Then comes the chapter, Block Designs: 12 Inches Square with 30 distinctive designs for patchwork blocks specially related to Christmas. All blocks are 12 inches square, which means that any block can be used interchangeably with the others. Some designs are traditional; these are presented with a selection of new designs, published here for the first time. From these designs you can create many different projects, which are featured in the climaxing chapter, Projects Based on 12-Inch-Square Blocks.

In Projects Based on 12-Inch-Square Blocks there are many options from pillows, quilts, and wall hangings to door decorations, table runners, and chair cushions. Choose your own theme. After selecting a project from this chapter, refer to the design section to pick the block or blocks of your choice. In this way, no projects will be alike and the finished items will be as different from one another as the people who made them.

Metric Equivalency Chart

mm—millimetres   cm—centimetres

INCHES TO MILLIMETRES AND CENTIMETRES

inches	mm	cm	inches	cm	inches	cm
⅛	3	0.3	9	22.9	30	76.2
¼	6	0.6	10	25.4	31	78.7
⅜	10	1.0	11	27.9	32	81.3
½	13	1.3	12	30.5	33	83.8
⅝	16	1.6	13	33.0	34	86.4
¾	19	1.9	14	35.6	35	88.9
⅞	22	2.2	15	38.1	36	91.4
1	25	2.5	16	40.6	37	94.0
1¼	32	3.2	17	43.2	38	96.5
1½	38	3.8	18	45.7	39	99.1
1¾	44	4.4	19	48.3	40	101.6
2	51	5.1	20	50.8	41	104.1
2½	64	6.4	21	53.3	42	106.7
3	76	7.6	22	55.9	43	109.2
3½	89	8.9	23	58.4	44	111.8
4	102	10.2	24	61.0	45	114.3
4½	114	11.4	25	63.5	46	116.8
5	127	12.7	26	66.0	47	119.4
6	152	15.2	27	68.6	48	121.9
7	178	17.8	28	71.1	49	124.5
8	203	20.3	29	73.7	50	127.0

YARDS TO METRES

yards	metres	yards	metres	yards	metres	yards	metres	yards	metres
⅛	0.11	2⅛	1.94	4⅛	3.77	6⅛	5.60	8⅛	7.43
¼	0.23	2¼	2.06	4¼	3.89	6¼	5.72	8¼	7.54
⅜	0.34	2⅜	2.17	4⅜	4.00	6⅜	5.83	8⅜	7.66
½	0.46	2½	2.29	4½	4.11	6½	5.94	8½	7.77
⅝	0.57	2⅝	2.40	4⅝	4.23	6⅝	6.06	8⅝	7.89
¾	0.69	2¾	2.51	4¾	4.34	6¾	6.17	8¾	8.00
⅞	0.80	2⅞	2.63	4⅞	4.46	6⅞	6.29	8⅞	8.12
1	0.91	3	2.74	5	4.57	7	6.40	9	8.23
1⅛	1.03	3⅛	2.86	5⅛	4.69	7⅛	6.52	9⅛	8.34
1¼	1.14	3¼	2.97	5¼	4.80	7¼	6.63	9¼	8.46
1⅜	1.26	3⅜	3.09	5⅜	4.91	7⅜	6.74	9⅜	8.57
1½	1.37	3½	3.20	5½	5.03	7½	6.86	9½	8.69
1⅝	1.49	3⅝	3.31	5⅝	5.14	7⅝	6.97	9⅝	8.80
1¾	1.60	3¾	3.43	5¾	5.26	7¾	7.09	9¾	8.92
1⅞	1.71	3⅞	3.54	5⅞	5.37	7⅞	7.20	9⅞	9.03
2	1.83	4	3.66	6	5.49	8	7.32	10	9.14

EQUIVALENT TERMS

American	British
muslin	calico
cheesecloth	cheesecloth or muslin

Making Patchwork Projects: Techniques

Selecting Fabrics & Threads

Each design is accompanied by a screened illustration, an assembly diagram and a list of templates that tells you how many pieces are needed and their suggested color or value (degree of light or dark): white, light, bright, medium, dark. Sometimes, I suggest the word "sky" or "striped" to indicate a color; it is up to you to select a suitable fabric. Follow the block lists, diagrams and illustrations exactly, or experiment with the placement of colors to create your own interpretation of each design.

Fabrics woven from 100-percent cotton threads are best for quiltmaking, although fabrics with some polyester content can be used. Don't use anything with less than 70-percent cotton, however. Select fabrics with highly contrasting values. Unorthodox combinations are fine and fun to use—especially in a Christmas project. Select an attractive interplay of solid fabrics (or fabrics with a tiny all-over print), fabrics with a medium-scale print and at least one with a large-scale print. Try to buy all fabrics for your project at the same time. You can best see how colors and patterns work with one another while they are still on the bolt. Matching fabrics from small scraps is very difficult and quite often doesn't work when you take the new selections home.

If in doubt about yardages, always buy *more* fabric than you think you'll need. Dye lots vary considerably; often, by the time you realize that you'll need more fabric, it may be too late to find the same dye lot. The fabric yardages listed for each project are exact and assume your cutting is precise. If you're not sure about the accuracy of your cutting, buy a little more fabric—you can always use the leftover pieces in some future creation.

When you are satisfied with your fabric choices, buy your sewing thread—an unobtrusive color that will blend with all the fabrics. Again, all-cotton thread is best, although cotton wrapped around a polyester core is fine.

Washing & Straightening

Prewash all fabrics to be used in your project. Wash the fabrics in the very hottest water and hang them to dry (tangling in a clothes dryer can twist the fabrics off-grain). Before putting the fabrics in the washing machine, clip into the selvages (finished edges) at 2-inch intervals to accommodate shrinkage. If there is any evidence that the fabric is not colorfast (the colors will bleed), wash the fabric again; or soak it in a solution of 3 parts cold water and 1 part white vinegar. Rinse the fabric and spread it on a white towel while wet. If there is still evidence of color bleeding, discard the fabric and select another. It is better to make this effort in the beginning than to experience the horror of washing a finished project only to find that it has been ruined by bleeding fabrics. If possible, iron the fabrics while they are slightly damp; the dampness makes it easier to remove all the wrinkles.

Check the grain. The crosswise and lengthwise threads of the fabric should be exactly perpendicular to each other. If they aren't perpendicular (and this is better when done with two pairs of hands), grasp the four corners of the fabric and pull diagonally from opposite corners simultaneously to straighten the grain. Repeat this pulling alternately from opposite corners until the threads are perpendicular to one another.

Prepare the fabrics for cutting as follows: Accurately cut off the selvages. To do this, measure an even distance from each finished edge (selvages are usually ¼ inch but can be as wide as ½ inch); draw a cutting line with a pencil and ruler. Cut away the selvages along the pencil line. Next, using a triangle and a ruler, draw a line across the fabric that is exactly perpendicular to the cut edge (Fig. 1). Cut away any excess fabric beyond this line. You are now ready to make your templates, mark your fabric and cut out your pieces.

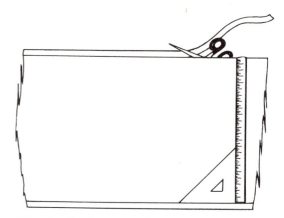

Fig. 1   Cutting away the selvages.

Making Templates & Cutting the Pieces

Using tracing paper and a pencil, trace the templates for the designs you have chosen. Mark each tracing with the name of the design, the letter of the template (the letter "I" is not used for templates in this book) and the value(s) of the fabric(s) from which it should be cut.

Glue the tracing to medium-weight cardboard or plastic; allow the glue to dry. Cut out each template using an X-acto knife or other cutting blade. For straight lines, use a straight metal edge to guide the knife.

The edge of the template is the sewing line; therefore, a ¼-inch seam allowance *must be added* when marking the templates on the fabric. The best way to do this is by drawing a ¼-inch seam allowance on the wrong side of the fabric along the lengthwise and crosswise cut edges (Fig. 2). You can then place the edge of your template on the marked line. Trace around the edge of your template. Use a ruler to mark a ¼-inch seam allowance around each of the remaining edges before marking the next template. Continue to mark all your templates on the wrong side of the fabric in this way.

To avoid waste and conserve fabric, mark your pieces so that they can be cut along a mutual edge (Fig. 3 and Fig. 4). As a rule, the longest edge of

any template should be placed on the straight (lengthwise) grain of the fabric. *All* edges of squares and rectangles should be on the straight grain.

Follow the list given with each design for the number of pieces to be cut and how to cut them. Symmetrical pieces do not need to be flipped over or "reversed," but many of the designs are made up of asymmetrical pieces; this need to reverse is always indicated with each list. When a design is asymmetrical and you are not instructed to reverse the template, it means the template has already been reversed for you. Where the list indicates a number of pieces are "reversed," turn your template over to the opposite (wrong) side and mark the necessary number of pieces on the fabric. You can check your work by studying the assembly diagram of your block.

After you have marked your pieces, carefully cut them out along the cutting lines. *Accuracy*—in both marking and cutting—is essential to the successful completion of each project. If you are cutting out all of your pieces at once, carefully gather and keep the pieces for each project in a separate envelope or plastic bag to avoid confusion when sewing time arrives.

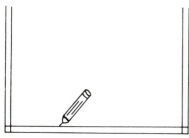

Fig. 2

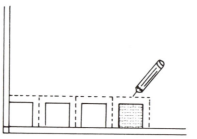

Fig. 3

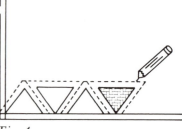

Fig. 4

Sewing the Pieces: Patchwork

I assume you will use a sewing machine to sew the pieces or patches for each project, although it is perfectly acceptable (though much slower) to do the piecing by hand.

Each design is accompanied by complete piecing instructions. Most designs are assembled in sub-units (squares, triangles, strips) that are then joined to complete the design.

When sewing pieces together, match the raw edges carefully, pinning them together at each end if necessary (Fig. 5). Sew the pieces together in chains

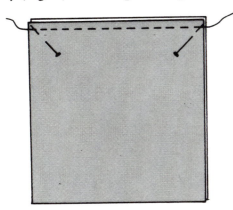

Fig. 5

to save time (Fig. 6). Always press the seams to one side, preferably towards the darker fabric (Fig. 7).

When sewing sub-units together, carefully match the seams before you sew, pinning the pieces at crucial points (Fig. 8). When matching seams, it is best to press seam allowances in opposite directions.

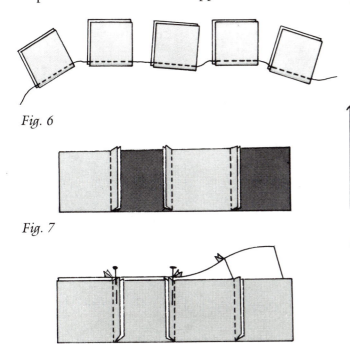

Fig. 6

Fig. 7

Fig. 8

HOW TO INSET

Sometimes, pieces of a design must be inset into one another. While this procedure is slightly tricky at first, it is possible to get perfect corners every time by using the following method:

1. A triangular or square piece is inset into two other pieces that are sewn together to form an angle (Fig. 9). When sewing those pieces together, end your stitching ¼-inch away from the edge to be inset (shown by the dot in the diagram).

2. Pin the piece to be inset along one edge of the angle (Fig. 10) and stitch from the middle (dot) to the edge (in the direction of the arrow).

3. Folding the excess fabric out of the way, pin the unsewn edges together and stitch from the central point to the outer edge (Fig. 11).

4. Open out the fabrics and carefully steam-press (Fig. 12). If you notice any puckers at the corner, you can usually eliminate them by removing a stitch from one of the seams just sewn.

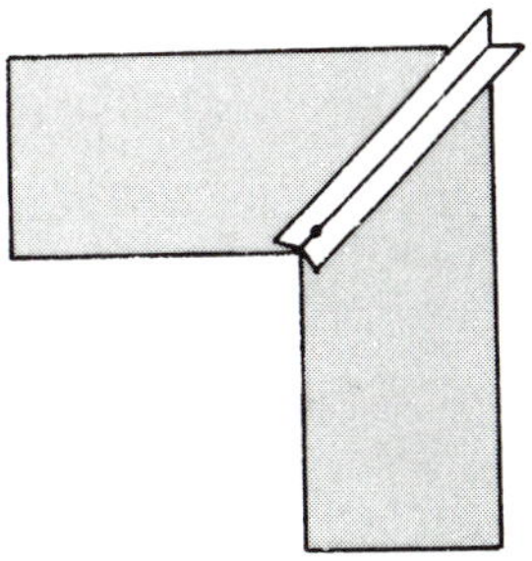

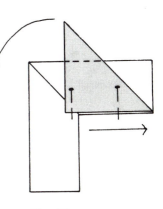

Fig. 9

Fig. 10

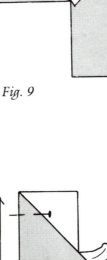

Fig. 11

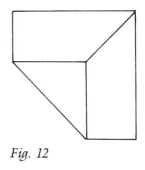

Fig. 12

SEWING CURVES

Curved edges are time-consuming to sew, but quite rewarding when finished. Excellent results can be achieved by following this procedure:

1. Clip the curve of the concave piece (Fig. 13).

2. Pin the clipped piece to the convex piece, matching the right angles at the corners first, then easing the curved edge to fit; stitch (Fig. 14).

3. Open out the fabrics and steam-press carefully (Fig. 15).

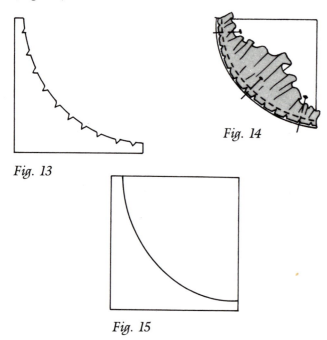

Fig. 13

Fig. 14

Fig. 15

HOW TO APPLIQUÉ

"Appliqué" means to apply to a larger surface, or in this technique, to apply one piece of fabric over another. While this book mainly features patchwork (or pieced) designs, there are some examples where appliquéing a tricky piece will make a design simple rather than challenging. The idea is to make the appliqué look like part of the patchwork. Other designs require small decorative touches to be appliquéd in place. Hand appliqué is recommended in both instances.

When cutting out the piece for each appliqué, be sure to add a ¼-inch seam allowance around the edges. Machine-stitch along the sewing line, using tiny stitches. Press the seam allowance to the wrong side, clipping into the seam allowance at curves and corners, where necessary, for ease; the machine stitches should be pressed just below the edge so that they are not visible. Baste the seam allowance in place, if desired.

Place the pressed appliqué in its correct position on your patchwork. Slip-stitch in place using tiny invisible stitches. Backstitch at the end to secure your thread.

Special Techniques

You can use special techniques to enhance or finish a project; these are referred to throughout the book.

RUFFLE

Cut the fabric strip to the required size, piecing the strip, if necessary, for additional length. With right sides together, stitch the short ends to each other (Fig. 16), forming a continuous circle of fabric. Fold the fabric in half lengthwise with wrong sides together and press; machine-baste ¼ inch away from the raw edges all around (Fig. 17). Gently pull the basting stitches, gathering the ruffle to approximately fit the edges of the project (Fig. 18). With raw edges meeting, pin the ruffle to the right side of the project, adjusting the gathers evenly to fit; allow extra gathers or make a pleat at each of the corners (Fig. 19). Stitch the ruffle securely to the project.

LACE

With raw edges meeting, pin the lace to the right side of the project; allow extra gathers or make a pleat at each of the corners (Fig. 19). Overlap the beginning and end of the lace by about ¼ inch; then stitch the lace securely to the project.

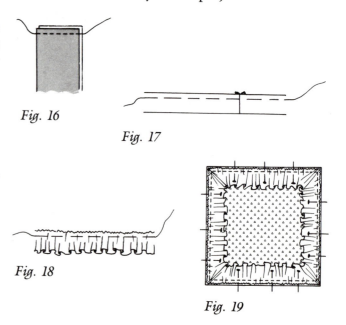

Fig. 16

Fig. 17

Fig. 18

Fig. 19

PIPING

Cut the fabric strip to the required size, piecing the strip, if necessary, for additional length. Place the piping cord on the middle of the wrong side of the fabric; then fold the fabric in half lengthwise, enclosing the piping cord. Using a zipper foot on the sewing machine, stitch close to the cord (Fig. 20).

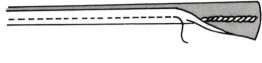

Fig. 20

Trim the seam allowance to ¼ inch. Pin the piping to the right side of the project with raw edges even. To ease the piping around each corner, clip into the seam allowance to the stitching line (Fig. 21). Continue pinning the piping in place until you reach the

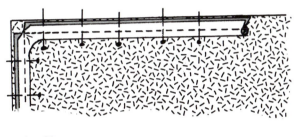

Fig. 21

beginning. Overlap the beginning of the piping by 1 inch; then cut away any excess. Remove 1 inch of stitching from the end of the piping, push back the excess fabric and trim away only the cord so that the beginning and end of the cord are flush (Fig. 22).

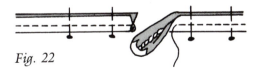

Fig. 22

Now straighten out the excess fabric and finger-press the raw edge ½ inch to the wrong side (inside) by running your finger over the fold a few times. Slip the beginning of the piping inside the end so that the excess fabric covers all raw edges (Fig. 23); pin in place. Stitch the piping to the project all around.

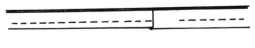

Fig. 23

EMBROIDERY

Hand embroidery can add a very special touch to a patchwork project. Often a few simple lines of embroidery can make a design come to life. Use any standard 6-strand cotton embroidery floss (thread).

If embroidery lines are given on a design, transfer the lines to the right side of your fabric using a hard lead pencil and graphite paper; or you can draw the design freehand on the fabric with a pencil.

Stretch the area to be embroidered in an embroidery hoop to hold the fabric taut; reposition the hoop as necessary while you are working. If the fabric sags in the hoop, pull it taut again. Embroider the design following the individual directions and stitch details (Fig. 24).

Outline stitch

Satin stitch **Straight stitch**

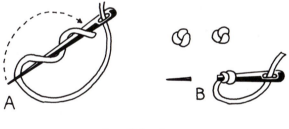 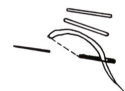

French knot

Fig. 24 Embroidery stitch details.

Each time you begin embroidering, leave extra thread dangling on the back of the fabric and embroider over it as you work to secure. Do not make knots. Hold the thread flat against the fabric with your free hand. To end a strand or begin a new one, weave the floss under the stitches on the back. From time to time, allow the needle and floss to hang straight down to unwind; this will prevent the floss from kinking or twisting while you embroider.

HOW TO MITRE CORNERS

Fold the raw ends of adjacent border or binding strips back on themselves to form a 45° angle (Fig. 25). Press. Pin and sew the edges together,

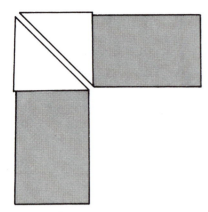

Fig. 26

Fig. 25

matching the creases formed by the pressing. Check the right side to make sure that the corner is perfect, with no puckers. If there are puckers, you can usually correct them by removing one of the stitches (as in step 4 of How to Inset). If the corner is perfect (Fig. 26), trim away the excess seam allowance, leaving a ¼-inch seam allowance. Press carefully.

LOOPS & TIES

Many of the projects in this book are meant to be hung or attached to something in some way. Loops and ties are made quickly and easily in a fabric that matches the binding.

Cut your chosen fabric to 2½ to 3 inches or the length indicated with your project. Press the strip in half lengthwise, wrong sides together. Open the strip and press each of the long raw edges exactly to the pressed central fold, again with the wrong sides together. Fold and press each of the short ends ¼ inch to the wrong side; then press the strip in half again, sandwiching all raw edges inside; topstitch the folded edges together. Attach the loops or ties to the project following the individual instructions.

Batting

Batting, the central core of a quilted project, is available in polyester, cotton, and wool. For washability and ease in handling, select a polyester batting; it can be purchased in many sizes and weights. It is best to use a thin batting for small projects to keep the puffiness in scale with the size of the finished design. A thicker batting can be used for larger projects, such as quilts and wall hangings or for designs that are quilted and then stuffed, such as pillows.

Cotton and wool battings are a bit more difficult to handle, but quilters who prefer pure natural fibres strongly recommend them. Projects made with cotton or wool battings must be quilted at 1½-inch intervals to prevent lumps from forming when the project is washed. It is best to dry-clean projects made with cotton or wool batting, however.

Assembling a Project for Quilting

A quilt is actually like a sandwich, with the batting as the filling and the top and back as the bread. To make the sandwich, you'll need a large flat surface, such as a large worktable or the floor.

Iron the back very well; tape it to the work surface, wrong side up, with the grain straight and all corners making 90° angles. Carefully place the batting over the middle of the lining. If you must piece

the batting, butt the edges and baste them together with large cross stitches.

Press the pieced top carefully—this will be the last time it will be ironed, so make the pressing a good one. Trim away any uneven seams on the back, and any threads or ravelled edges. When you are satisfied, set the top, right side up, over the batting to match the outside edges.

Baste the three layers together quite thoroughly: first baste diagonally from the middle to each corner, then crosswise and lengthwise (Fig. 27). If you are using a quilting frame, put the quilt into the frame. If quilting with a hoop, add some additional basting (concentric squares) for extra safety.

You are now ready to quilt.

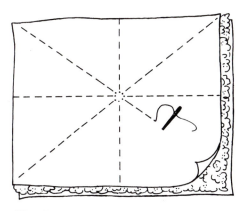

Fig. 27

How to Quilt

You'll need a quilting or "between" needle, size 7 through 10 (10 is the smallest); an 8 needle is a good size for most quilters. A thimble for the middle finger of your sewing hand is essential as is strong and mercerized 100-percent cotton quilting thread. Some quilters like to use a second thimble on the index finger of the hand under the quilt; this is optional.

To begin, cut an 18-inch length of quilting thread; thread your needle and knot the end of the thread. Run the needle and thread through the pieced top and some of the batting, pulling the knot beneath the surface of the quilt top (it usually makes a satisfying "popping" sound) and burying it in the batting (Fig. 28).

The quilting stitch is basically a running stitch. Hold the index finger of your left hand (for right-handed quilters) or right hand (for left-handed quilters) beneath the project just below the spot where you wish to make your stitches. Try to achieve a smooth rhythm, rocking your needle from the surface to the back, and then returning it again to the surface. Try to make 3 to 4 stitches at a time. Fig. 29 shows how to use the thimble to help push the needle through the fabric; the illustration also shows how the finger beneath pushes against the project to compress the batting, making it easier to take several stitches at a time. Fig. 30 is a cross-section diagram showing how the quilting stitches should look when done correctly.

Don't panic if your stitches look larger than you think they should—an *even line* of stitches is the important procedure, not the size of the stitches. The more you quilt, the smaller your stitches will become, but in the beginning, concentrate on making the stitches the same length on the top and on the back.

Suggestions for how to quilt each project are given at the end of each set of piecing instructions.

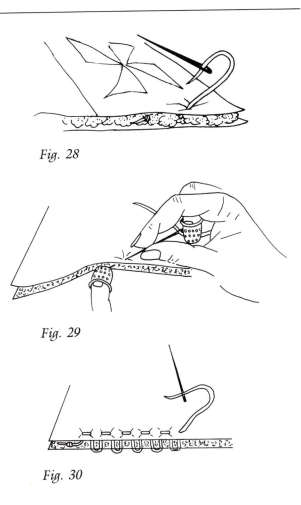

Fig. 28

Fig. 29

Fig. 30

For more quilting ideas, see Fig. 31 and also the finished projects shown on the color pages.

If you are using a hoop, baste strips of fabric, 6 to 12 inches wide, to the edges of the project so that it can be held in the hoop when you are quilting the outer edges.

In addition to the traditional type of quilting just described, two other methods are used to quilt some of the projects in this book: the tufting stitch, and the quilt-as-you-go method. Follow the instructions below for each method.

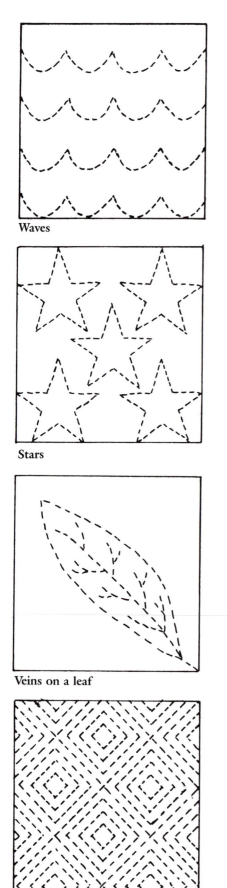
Waves

Stars

Veins on a leaf

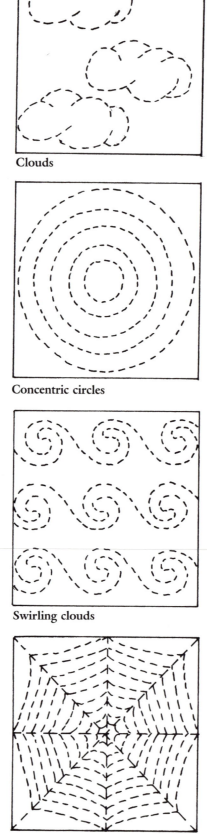
Clouds

Concentric circles

Swirling clouds

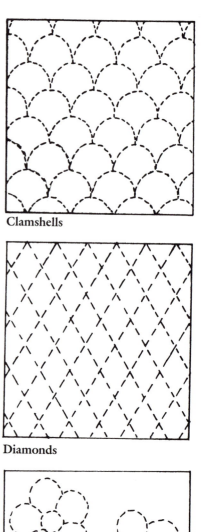
Clamshells

Diamonds

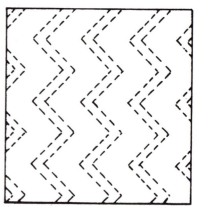
Flowers

Concentric diamonds

Spider web

Zigzag

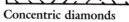

Fig. 31   Quilting design ideas.

18

TUFTING STITCH

The tufting stitch can be used on the right or wrong side of a project, depending upon whether or not you wish the knot to show. Following Fig. 32 and using a length of quilting thread, make a backstitch through all 3 layers of the project (1); the ends should be even (2). Tie the ends in a simple knot (3); tie another knot over the first (4). Pull tight and trim the ends close to the knot (5).

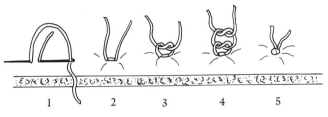

Fig. 32 Tufting stitch.

QUILT-AS-YOU-GO METHOD

Use the quilt-as-you-go technique for simple patchwork designs; piecing and quilting are done at the same time using a sewing machine. This method considerably shortens the time needed to make a project because when the sewing is done, the project is finished (except for the binding).

Follow the requirements for the project you are making to cut the back and batting pieces; the batting should be ¼-inch smaller than the back at each edge. Place the batting on the middle of the wrong side of the back; baste in place diagonally or horizontally and vertically so that the threads will cross in the exact middle of the block; these lines will serve as guidelines for placement of the patchwork. Place the basted piece, batting side up, on a flat surface. Position the first patchwork piece, right side up, on the batting and baste in place all around (Fig. 33). Pin the second piece over the first with right sides together and raw edges even. Stitch together ¼ inch from the edge, making sure all the layers feed smoothly under the presser foot of the sewing machine (Fig. 34). Remove the pins and fold the second piece to the right side; finger-press by running your finger over the seam a few times

(Fig. 35). (Do not be tempted to use an iron for pressing or you may be faced with melted batting!) Continue adding pieces, as directed, until the entire base is covered, finger-pressing after each new piece is added. Complete the project, following the individual instructions.

When the quilting is finished, remove your basting stitches. You are now ready for the final step—the binding.

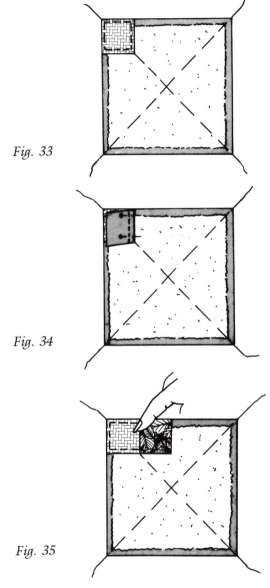

Fig. 33

Fig. 34

Fig. 35

Binding a Project

The binding is the finishing touch to your project and should be used to enhance the overall design; give it careful consideration. All project requirements include the measurements for a separate binding, although many of the projects can be finished with self-binding or fold-finishing (see below). Usually, the binding is cut on the straight grain of the fabric, but there are times when the binding must be cut on the bias. While I usually do not recommend using a purchased binding, for a small project, such as a stocking or pot holder, it would be far easier—and much quicker!—to use double-fold bias tape.

SEPARATE BINDING

A separate binding takes a bit more time to prepare than a self-binding, but it gives you the freedom to choose any preferred color or print.

To prepare a separate binding, cut your chosen fabric to the length indicated with the requirements for your project. For a large project, such as a quilt, piecing will be necessary. Press the strip in half lengthwise, wrong sides together. Open the strip and press one long raw edge exactly to the pressed central fold, again with the wrong sides together; this folded edge is later slip-stitched to the back of the project.

With right sides together and raw edges even, pin the unpressed edge of the binding to the right side of the project. If you are binding a quilt, allow extra fabric at each corner for mitring. For most other projects, about ¼ inch excess fabric should extend beyond each edge of the piece you are binding; this excess fabric is later folded under to conceal the raw edges.

Stitching binding to a quilt with a border: To conceal the raw edges, fold under one end of the binding ¼ inch (the beginning) and overlap with the other (the end). Make a ½-inch seam and turn stitching sharply at each corner. When you have bound the whole quilt, trim away any excess binding, if necessary. You do not have to fold under the end of the binding; just make sure it overlaps the beginning by about ½ inch. Wrap the pressed edge of the binding over the raw edges of the quilt to the back; slip-stitch invisibly, and mitre the corners.

Stitching binding to a quilted project: Start your stitching at the edge and stitch to the opposite edge, making a ¼-inch seam. Wrap the pressed edge of the binding over the raw edges of the project to the back; slip-stitch invisibly in place, folding the excess fabric at each end to the wrong side to conceal the raw edges. Complete each strip of binding in turn before adding the next one.

SELF-BINDING

Self-binding is a quick and easy way to finish a quilted project. This technique is not always recommended when the back is made from the same fabric as the border because of the effect; self-binding can make the edges of the project seem to fade away,

particularly if the colors of the project are very strong.

If you decide to self-bind your project, mark and cut an extra inch all around the edge of the fabric for the back; this will add 2 inches to the length and width measurements. (Most projects include fabric for a self-binding in the measurements given for the back.) Arrange the batting and top carefully over the lining to leave the inch-wide border free around the edges.

After the quilting is done, you can bind the project. Finger-press the edges of the back ½ inch inward to the wrong side of the fabric to make a folded edge. Then wrap the back towards the pieced top, covering the edges of the batting and top. Pin the folded edge to the top (Fig. 36). Slip-stitch the

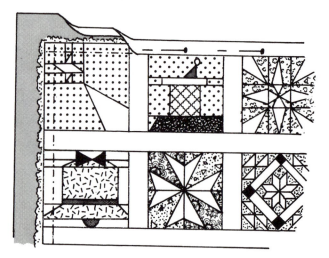

Fig. 36

folded edge of the back invisibly to the top. Mitre the corners or conceal the raw ends, as necessary. Remove all pins when finished.

FOLD-FINISHING

This type of "binding" should be done *before* the project has been quilted. Trim the raw edges of the back even with the top; then fold the raw edges of both the top and back ¼ inch towards each other to conceal the raw edges inside the project. Slip-stitch together invisibly and securely. To quilt, baste strips of muslin to the finished edge of the project so that it can be placed in a frame or hoop.

Your Signature

Your project will have greater personal and historic value if it is signed and dated. Embroider your name and the date on the front or back with embroidery floss or sign your name and date on the back with indelible ink.

Quick Holiday Gifts
& Decorations

PATCHWORK WREATHS

A festive wreath on a front door is always a welcoming sight during the holiday season. This year, make a patchwork wreath to greet your Christmas guests.

Finished size: 15" diameter

Requirements

Patchwork front: 1   15½" diameter—3 fabrics, ¼ yard each

Back: 1   15½ diameter—½ yard

Polyester fibrefill

Satin ribbon: ½" wide—2 yards

Select one of the following wreath designs; piece as directed in the individual instructions. After the patchwork front has been completed, use it as a pattern to cut the fabric for the back. For the central opening, cut away the backing fabric, leaving an extra ½-inch allowance all around. Clip into the seam allowance of the front and back to the stitching line at regular intervals all around the inner opening.

With right sides together, pin the front to the back; stitch together around the outer edges, making a ¼-inch seam. Clip into the seam allowance at each corner just to the stitching line. Turn to the right side and press. Press the inner seam allowance of the front (only) ¼ inch to the wrong side.

Begin stuffing the interior of the wreath evenly all around from the inner opening. As the wreath becomes plump, pin the pressed edges of the front over the back, matching the stitching lines. Continue stuffing as you pin, until the wreath is quite firm. Slip-stitch the front securely to the back all around the central opening with matching thread.

Sew a hook to the back of the wreath. Make a pretty bow with the satin ribbon and tack to the front of the wreath; trim the ends of the ribbon at an angle.

Star Wreath

(Color page 70)

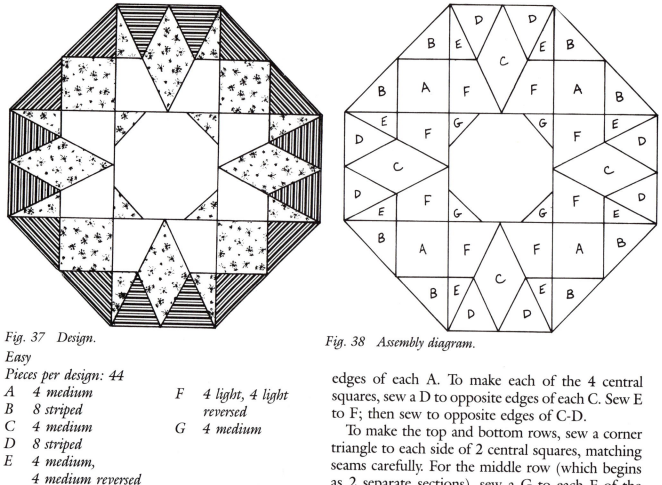

Fig. 37   Design.

Fig. 38   Assembly diagram.

Easy

Pieces per design: 44

A   4 medium

B   8 striped

C   4 medium

D   8 striped

E   4 medium,
    4 medium reversed

F   4 light, 4 light
    reversed

G   4 medium

Assemble the wreath in 3 horizontal rows. To make each of the 4 corner triangles, sew 2 B's to adjacent edges of each A. To make each of the 4 central squares, sew a D to opposite edges of each C. Sew E to F; then sew to opposite edges of C-D.

To make the top and bottom rows, sew a corner triangle to each side of 2 central squares, matching seams carefully. For the middle row (which begins as 2 separate sections), sew a G to each F of the remaining squares, as shown. Sew the 3 rows together, matching seams carefully, to complete the design.

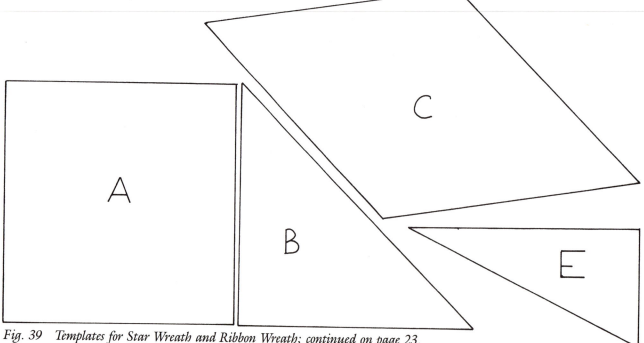

Fig. 39   Templates for Star Wreath and Ribbon Wreath; continued on page 23.

22

Ribbon Wreath

(Color page 70)

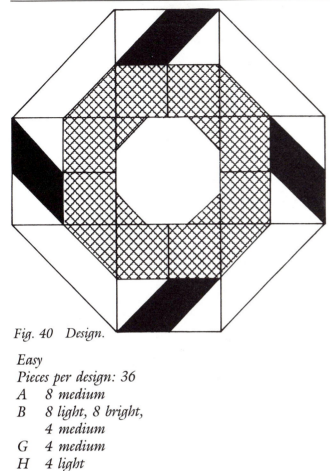

Fig. 40   Design.

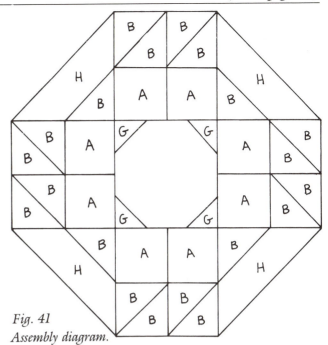

Fig. 41
Assembly diagram.

Easy
Pieces per design: 36
A   *8 medium*
B   *8 light, 8 bright,*
    4 medium
G   *4 medium*
H   *4 light*

Assemble the wreath in 3 horizontal rows. To make each of the 4 corner triangles, sew a medium B to each H. To make each of the 4 central squares, sew 4 pairs of A's together. Sew a light B to each bright B, making 8 squares; sew 4 pairs of B-B squares together, matching the bright B's as shown. Sew each A-A to B-B.

To make the top and bottom rows, sew a corner triangle to each side of 2 central squares, matching seams carefully. For the middle row (which begins as 2 separate sections), sew a G to each A of the remaining squares, as shown. Sew the 3 rows together, matching seams carefully, to complete the design.

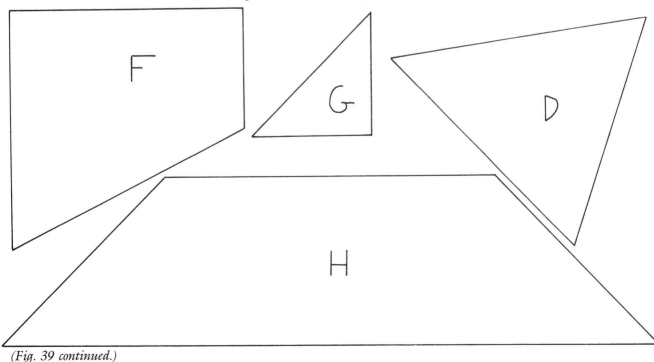

(Fig. 39 continued.)

TREE ORNAMENTS

Complete with Christmas carols and delicious egg-nog, the ceremony of trimming the tree is a very important tradition in my family. Every year a new ornament is carefully made or chosen and added to our splendid collection.

Why not begin your own tradition and make a lovely patchwork ornament to commemorate each Christmas? Select from the charming designs described below; some are shown on the color pages. Use up your bright fabric scraps, bits of lace, and piping to make each creation a unique treasure. If you have time, make a special ornament to decorate your Christmas packages. Your friends will be delighted with the extra little gift!

Each ornament can be filled with fibrefill, potpourri, or even pine needles. Don't stop at Christmas. To use as sachets or pincushions throughout the year, make them in non-Christmas fabrics.

To make an ornament, select one of these designs and piece, as directed in the individual instructions. Using the pieced front as a pattern, cut the back from a scrap of matching fabric. Decide on the finish you'd like to use: ruffled fabric, lace, piping or plain. You will need approximately ½ yard of lace or piping, or a strip of fabric (1½ by 24 inches) for the ruffle to complete each ornament.

Ruffled fabric: Press the strip of fabric you cut for the ruffle. With right sides together, stitch the short ends, forming a continuous circle of fabric. With wrong sides together, fold the fabric in half lengthwise and press; machine-baste ¼ inch from the raw edges all around (Fig. 42). Gently pull the basting stitches and gather the ruffle to approximately fit the edges of the ornament (Fig. 43). With raw edges

Fig. 42   Machine-baste the ruffle.

Fig. 43   Gather the ruffle.

even, pin the ruffle to the right side of the ornament, adjusting the gathers evenly to fit; allow extra gathers or make a pleat at each corner (Fig. 44). Stitch the ruffle securely to the ornament, making a ⅛-inch seam.

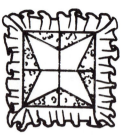

Fig. 44   Ruffle finish.

Lace: With raw edges even, pin the lace to the right side of the ornament; make a pleat at each corner (Fig. 45). Overlap the ends of the lace by about ¼ inch. Stitch the lace securely to the ornament, making a ⅛-inch seam.

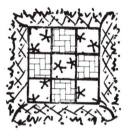

Fig. 45   Lace finish.

Piping: See Ruffle and Piping for instructions on preparing and sewing it to the ornament.

After the ruffle, lace, or piping has been added, pin the front to the back with right sides together, raw edges even, and any ruffles, lace, or piping sandwiched in between. Stitch together, ¼ inch from the edges, leaving a 1½-inch opening for turning. (For a *plain finish*, simply stitch the front and back together as described.) Clip off each corner at an angle—unless, of course, you are making round ornaments; then turn to the right side. Stuff with fibrefill until plump. Slip-stitch the opening to close it. Cut a ¼-yard length of ribbon or lace; tie into a decorative knot or bow and slip-stitch to the top of the ornament, making a loop for hanging.

Fig. 46   Piping finish.

Fig. 47   Plain finish.

24

Morning Star

Fig. 48 Design.

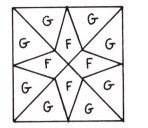

Fig. 49 Assembly diagram.

Easy
Finished size: 4" × 4"
Pieces per ornament: 12
F   4 medium
G   4 bright, 4 bright
*   reversed*

Sew a G to each side of each F. Sew 2 F-G triangles together to make each half; sew the halves together, matching seams carefully, to complete the design. To add dimension to the ornament, make a tufting stitch through the front, batting, and back at the midpoint of the star; see Tufting Stitch.

Nine-Patch Ornament   *(Color page 66)*

Fig. 50   Design.   Fig. 51   Assembly diagram.

Easy
Finished size: 3" × 3"
Pieces per ornament: 9
A   4 light, 5 bright
*   (or any*
*   combination)*

Feature any whimsical fabric prints you may have on this ornament: teddy bears, cats, trees, or toys that tell a special story. Assemble the ornament in 3 rows with 3 squares in each row; match seams carefully when sewing the rows together. For a special tufted effect, make a tufting stitch at each corner of the central square through the front, batting, and back; see Tufting Stitch.

Bright Star

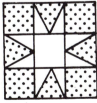

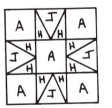

Fig. 52   Design.   Fig. 53   Assembly diagram.

Easy
Finished size: 3" × 3"
Pieces per ornament: 17
A   1 light, 4 bright   J   4 bright
H   4 light, 4 light
*   reversed*

Sew an H to adjacent edges of each J, as shown. Sew an H-J-H piece to each opposite side of the light A. Sew a bright A to each H of the remaining H-J-H pieces; then sew to the top and bottom of H-A-H, matching seams carefully.

For a lovely dimensional effect, make a tufting stitch through the front, batting, and back at the corners of the central A; see Tufting Stitch.

Twinkling Star

(Color page 67)

Fig. 54   Design.

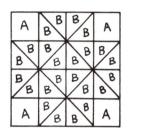

Fig. 55   Assembly diagram.

Easy
Finished size: 4" × 4"
Pieces per ornament: 28
A   4 bright
B   4 light, 10 bright,
     10 dark

Arrange the pieces as shown in the diagram; then sew all the B triangles together to form squares. Sew the A and B-B squares together in 4 rows with 4 squares in each row. Sew the rows together, matching seams carefully, to complete the design. For a special effect, make a tufting stitch at each corner of each light B and another in the middle; sew through the front, batting, and back; see Tufting Stitch.

Variable Star

(Color page 67)

Fig. 56   Design.

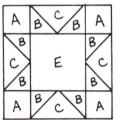

Fig. 57   Assembly diagram.

Easy
Finished size: 4" × 4"
Pieces per ornament: 17
A   4 bright   C   4 bright
B   8 medium   E   1 medium

Sew a B to adjacent edges of each C, as shown. Sew a B-C-B piece to opposite sides of E. Sew an A to each B of the remaining B-C-B pieces; then sew to B-E-B, matching seams carefully.

For a lovely dimensional effect, make a tufting stitch through the front, batting, and back at each corner of E; see Tufting Stitch.

Radiant Star

Fig. 58   Design.

Fig. 59   Assembly diagram.

Challenging
Finished size: 4" × 4"
Pieces per ornament: 21
O   1 light   R   4 medium
P   4 light   S   4 bright
Q   4 medium,
     4 medium reversed

See How to Inset before beginning. Sew a Q to adjacent edges of each P, matching the large dots. Sew an R to the remaining edge of each P. Sew the Q edges of each triangle to O. Inset S into each angle formed by the arms of the star.

Shooting Star

Fig. 60 Design.

Fig. 61 Assembly diagram.

Medium
Finished size: 4" × 4"
Pieces per ornament: 24

T 4 light	V 4 dark
U 4 bright, 4 bright reversed	W 4 bright, 4 bright reversed

Sew a U to adjacent edges of each T, as shown; then sew a W to adjacent edges of each V in the same manner. Sew each T-U section to a V-W section, making 4 quarters of the design. Sew the quarters together for each half; then sew the halves together, matching seams carefully in the middle, to complete the design.

Lemon Star

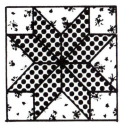

Fig. 62 Design.

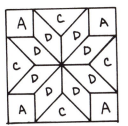

Fig. 63 Assembly diagram.

Challenging
Finished size: 4" × 4"
Pieces per ornament: 16

A 4 bright	D 4 medium,
C 4 bright	4 medium reversed

See How to Inset before beginning. Sew each D piece to its reverse, forming 4 pairs of star points. Sew 2 pairs of star points together to make each half of the star; press the central seams of each half in opposite directions to reduce bulk. Sew the star halves together, matching seams in the middle. Inset the A and C pieces between the star points to form a square.

For a lovely dimensional effect, make a tufting stitch through the front, batting, and back at the midpoint of the star; see Tufting Stitch.

Amish Shadowed Square

(Color page 66)

Fig. 64 Design.

Fig. 65 Assembly diagram.

Easy
Finished size: 4" × 4"
Pieces per ornament: 5

X   1 light
Y, Z, A1, B   assorted
                   fabrics

Sew B to A1, A1 to Z and Z to Y to complete the pieced half of the square. Sew the long edges of X and Y together to complete the design.

Evergreen

Fig. 66 Design.

Fig. 67 Assembly diagram.

Easy
Finished size: 3" × 3"
Pieces per ornament: 6

| K | 1 medium | M | 1 dark |
| L | 1 bright, 1 bright reversed | N | 2 bright |

Sew an L to each side of K; sew an N to each side of M. Sew K to N-M-N to complete the design.

Bow

(Color page 67)

Fig. 68 Design.

Fig. 69 Assembly diagram.

Easy
Finished size: 3" diameter
Pieces per ornament: 6

| B | 2 bright | J1 | 2 medium |
| H1 | 2 light | | |

Sew each B to an H1. Sew an H-B to each J1, making the 2 halves. Sew the halves together to complete the design.

Shining Star

(Color page 67)

Fig. 70 Design.

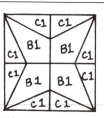

Fig. 71 Assembly diagram.

Easy
Finished size: 3" × 3"
Pieces per ornament: 12

B1 4 light
C1 4 bright, 4 bright reversed

Sew a C1 to each side of each B1. Sew 2 B-C squares together to make each half; sew the halves together to complete the design.

Wreath

(Color page 67)

Fig. 72 Design.

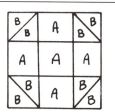

Fig. 73 Assembly diagram.

Easy
Finished size: 3" × 3"
Pieces per ornament: 13

| A | 1 light, 4 dark | B | 4 light, 4 dark |

Sew each light B to a dark B, making the 4 corner squares. Sew the B-B and A squares together in 3 rows with 3 squares in each row, as shown in the diagram. Sew the rows together, matching seams carefully, to complete the design.

String Tree

(Color page 67)

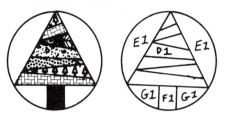

Fig. 74 Design.   Fig. 75 Assembly diagram.

Easy
Finished size: 3" diameter
Pieces per ornament: 6

D1 1 bright	G1 1 light, 1 light
E1 2 light	reversed
F1 1 dark	

This ornament would be quite pretty if the tree were cut from only one fabric; to make it special, however, sew strips of various fabrics across the D1 piece to make it look like a "string" tree. Here's how to do it: Using the diagram as a guide, cut 7 strips of fabric in varying widths for the tree. Angled diagonally, place the first strip, right side up, at about the middle of D1; stitch each long edge in place to fasten to D1. With wrong sides together, stitch a strip to each opposite edge of the first strip; press

these strips to their right sides. You now have 3 different strips: the middle with finished edges sewn on the tree, and the 2 outer strips with their outer edges still unfinished. Continue adding strips to the unfinished edges in this manner until the tree is completely covered. Trim away the excess strips on each side, even with edges of D1.

Sew an E1 to each side of D1. Sew a G1 to each side of F1; sew the strip just made to the bottom of D1 to complete the design.

Treetop Star

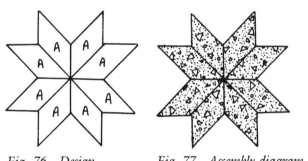

Fig. 76 Design.   Fig. 77 Assembly diagram.

Easy
Pieces per design: 8
A   4 bright, 4 bright
     reversed

Your Christmas tree will be complete with a star at the top. Make this simple star with a scrap of glittery gold or red fabric. Use template A; some fibrefill and a small piece of ½-inch elastic are the only other supplies needed to complete the project.

Sew each A piece to its reverse to make 4 pairs. Sew 2 pairs together, forming each half of the star; press the central seams of each half in opposite directions to reduce bulk at the junction. Sew the halves of the star together, matching the seams in the middle. Press carefully; then use the pieced star as a pattern to cut the back.

With right sides of the front and back together

and raw edges even, stitch around the outside edges, turning your stitching sharply at each point and at each angle between the points; leave a 2-inch opening to turn the star right side out later. Trim off the seam allowance at each point, close to the stitching. Clip into the seam allowance at each angle just to the stitching line. Turn to the right side. Stuff with fibrefill until plump; then slip-stitch the opening to close. Slip-stitch the ends of a 1½-inch piece of elastic to the back of the star to make a holder; slip the top branch of the tree into the elastic holder and adjust the star in place.

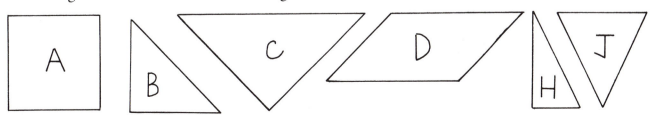

Fig. 78 Templates for Tree Ornaments; continued on page 30.

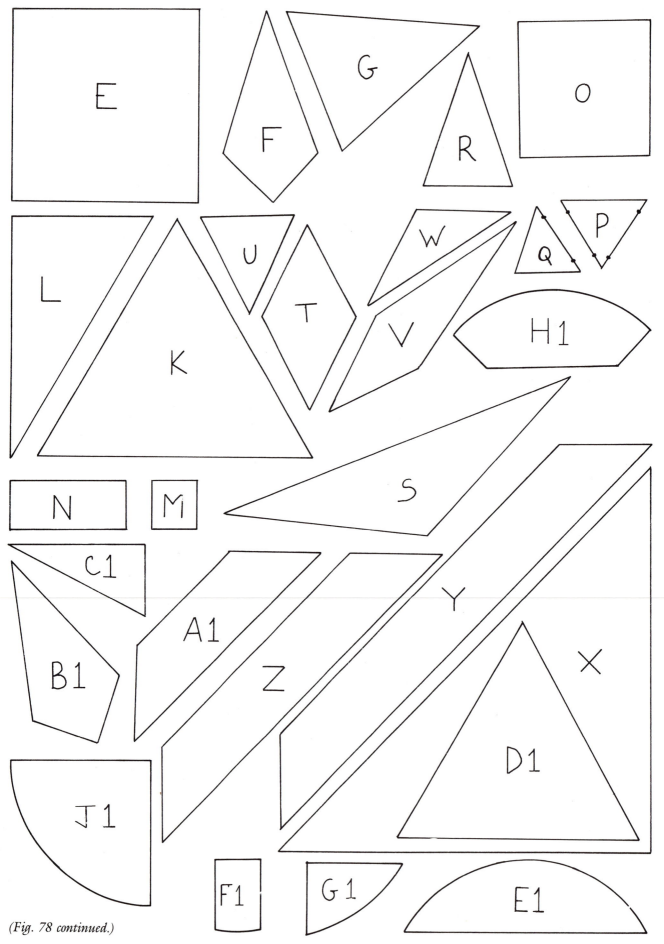

(Fig. 78 continued.)

30

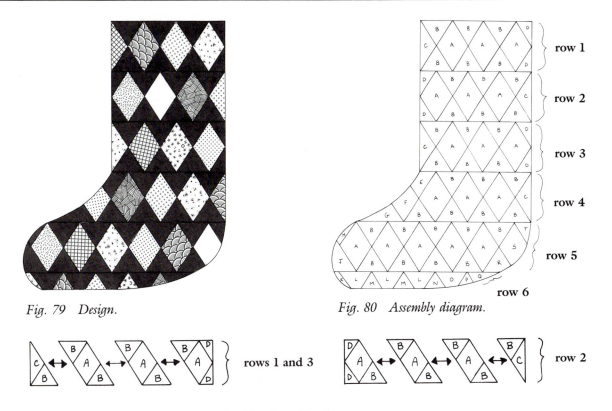

Fig. 79   Design.

Fig. 80   Assembly diagram.

Fig. 81   Assembly of rows.

Finished size: about 13" × 16"
Requirements
Bright fabric: ½ yard
Assorted fabrics: scraps
Batting: 1   13" × 16"
Back and lining: 2   13" × 16"—½ yard
Double-fold bias seam binding: 3 yards
Easy
Pieces per design: 79

A	17 assorted	K	1 assorted
B	34 bright	L	3 bright
C	4 assorted	M	2 assorted
D	3 bright, 3 bright reversed	N	1 assorted
		O	1 bright
E	1 bright	P	1 assorted
F	1 assorted	Q	1 bright
G	1 bright	R	1 bright
H	1 bright	S	1 assorted
J	1 bright	T	1 bright

Hang this stocking by your chimney with care for some special treats every Christmas! It is very easy to make. The dynamic zigzag effect of the bright pieces will be heightened by the printed motifs you feature in each diamond.

Assemble the stocking in 6 horizontal rows. On a flat surface, arrange the pieces, as shown in the assembly diagram to get a pleasing mix of the assorted fabrics for the diamond shapes. When satisfied with your arrangement, separate the pieces into 6 rows.

Each of the rows is pieced in diagonal strips; the strips are then sewn together, with the points of the diamonds and triangles matching. Follow Fig. 81 to stitch the diagonal strips for rows 1 and 3; join the diagonal strips, matching the points indicated by the arrows. Follow Fig. 81 to stitch row 2 in the same manner. Continue in the same way to sew rows 4, 5, and 6, using pieces E to T to shape the foot, as shown in the diagram. Stitch the rows together, following the diagram, to complete the front of the stocking.

Use the pieced front as a pattern to cut the batting, lining and back pieces; be sure to cut the lining and back in reverse to the front. See instructions on Assembling a Project for Quilting; assemble the top, batting, and lining. Hand- or machine-quilt the outlines of the zigzag patterns formed by the bright pieces.

With wrong sides together and raw edges even, make a ⅛-inch seam and stitch the quilted front to the back, leaving the top edge open. Finish the raw edges of the stocking with double-fold bias seam binding: Unfold one side of the binding, and with right sides together and raw edges even, stitch to the stocking front in one continuous strip, sewing along the fold line of the binding; start at the top back edge and end at the top front. Wrap the binding over the raw edges of the stocking, easing around the curved areas, and slip-stitch to the back with matching thread. Bind the top of the stocking in the same manner, folding under the ends so there are no raw edges. Make a 3-inch loop with a scrap of binding and slip-stitch the ends inside the stocking at the top back edge.

Fig. 82 Templates for Argyle Stocking.

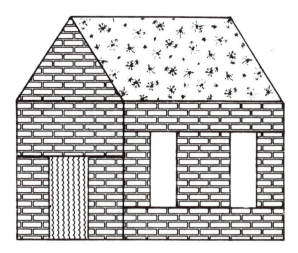

Fig. 83   Design.

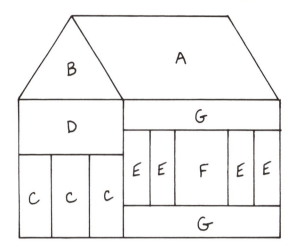

Fig. 84   Assembly diagram.

Easy
Finished size: 8" × 10"
Pieces per design: 13

A	*1 white or brown*	*B*	*1 bright*
	(follow the solid	*C*	*2 bright, 1 striped*
	line for the	*D*	*1 bright*
	doorstop, the dash	*E*	*2 light, 2 bright*
	line for the wall	*F*	*1 bright*
	hanging)	*G*	*2 bright*

Add a festive touch to some of your doors by propping them open with this elegant doorstop. For year-round use, make the roof in a dark brown fabric and the windows yellow or white. For holiday use, cut the roof of white eyelet or embroidered fabric to resemble snow, and display a Christmas tree in one of the windows, as shown in the photograph. Scraps of fabric, some fibrefill, and sand are the only other supplies needed to complete this easy project.

To do the patchwork, sew B to the left edge of A. Sew a bright C to each side of the striped C; sew D to C-C-C. For the window strip, sew a light E to each long side of F; sew a bright E to each light E. Sew G to the top and bottom of the window strip; then sew G-E-G to D-C. Sew B-A to D-G to complete the design.

Finishing: Use the pieced front to cut a back in reverse from a scrap of fabric. With right sides together and raw edges even, stitch the front to the back leaving a 3-inch opening along the top edge. Turn to the right side and fill with a mixture of fibrefill and sand, padding the roof and sides carefully with fibrefill to prevent drooping. (Or you can also use fibrefill and some lead weights.) When the doorstop is full, turn the raw edges at the opening ¼-inch inside and slip-stitch the opening to close.

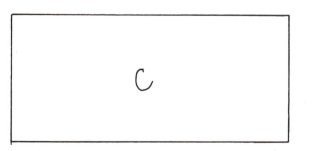

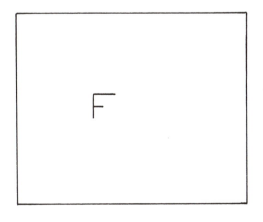

Fig. 85   Templates for House Doorstop; continued on page 34.

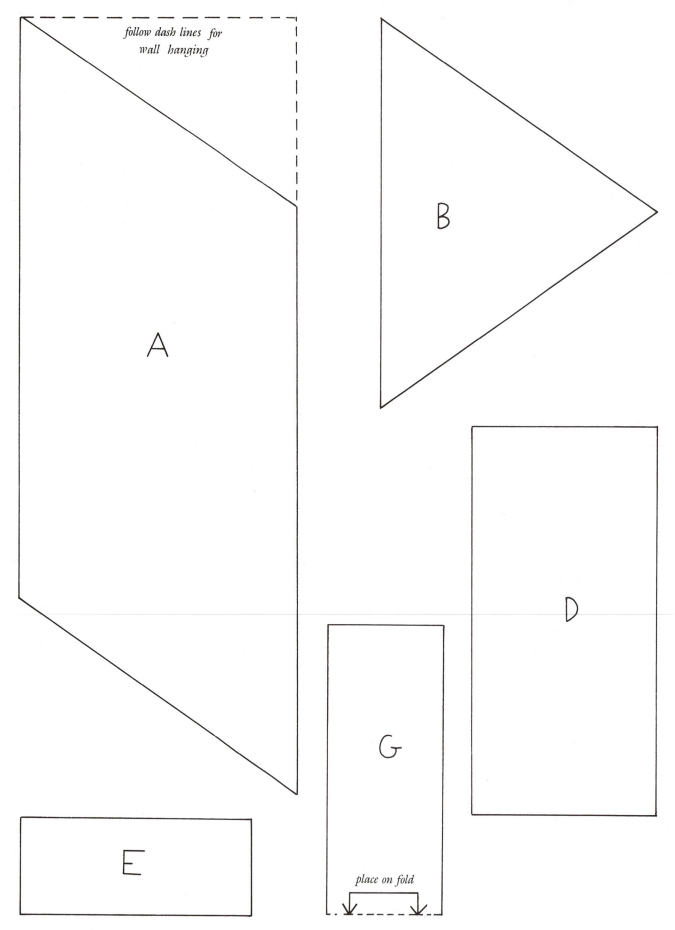

follow dash lines for wall hanging

A

B

D

G

place on fold

E

(*Fig. 85 continued.*)

34

Tote Bags

Finished size: 12" × 16" × 4"
Requirements
Pieced blocks: 24   4" square—¼ yard each of 3 to 8 fabrics*
Back (for quilting): 2   12½" × 16½"—⅜ yard muslin
Remainder of bag: 1 yard
Front/back linings: 2   12½" × 16½"
Piping fabric: 2   1" × 68"
Side panels: 2   4" × 16½"
Side panel linings: 2   4" × 16½"
Base: 1   4" × 12½"
Base lining: 1   4" × 12½"
Top edge lining: 1   1½" × 33"
Straps: 2   3½" × 24"
Piping cord: ¼" diameter—4 yards
Batting: 2   12" × 16"
Interfacing: 2   3½" × 24"—¼ yard
*The Lattice design requires only 3 different fabrics, while the Whirling Poinsettia design requires 8 fabrics.

Here's a sturdy tote bag—and two striking designs—to use for any shopping expedition, especially when Christmas shopping. The Lattice design, an intriguing puzzle, will dazzle other Christmas shoppers; bright and cheery Whirling Poinsettias is full of movement and color.

Select the Lattice or Whirling Poinsettias design; piece 24 blocks, as directed in the individual instructions. Each side of the tote bag has 12 pieced blocks. After all the blocks are complete, arrange them in 4 rows with 3 blocks in each row, following the assembly diagram. Sew together in horizontal rows, matching seams carefully. Sew the rows together to complete the front. Construct the back in the same manner.

See Assembling a Project for Quilting and assemble the front and back as directed; then quilt the pieces, following the individual instructions.

To make the piping, cut 2 lengths of piping cord, each 68 inches. Review Piping for instructions on making and attaching the piping; then attach the piping to the front and back.

You can now attach the side panels. With right sides together, raw edges even, and the piping sandwiched between the panels, using a zipper foot, sew one long edge of each side panel to each long edge of the pieced front, sewing close to the piping. Attach the back to the remaining long edges of the side panels in the same manner.

Next, attach the base. With right sides together and raw edges even, sew the 12½-inch sides of the base to the pieced front and back; again, the piping will be sandwiched between the layers. Finally, stitch the 4-inch edges of the base to each of the side panels.

To line the sides and base, press the raw edges of the lining pieces ¼ inch to the wrong side. Pin over the seams on the inside of the tote bag, hiding the raw edges at the sides and bottom; slip-stitch invisibly in place, leaving the top edges raw. If desired, sew a long dart in each of the side panels, making the dart ¼-inch deep at the top and tapering to nothing near the base. This will secure the lining to the sides and will cause the sides to fold inward naturally.

Attach the top edge lining next. Press one short and one long edge of the strip ¼ inch to the wrong side. With right sides together and raw edges even, pin the other long edge all around the top edge of the bag; pin the raw short end over the pressed end so there will be no raw edges when the lining is turned inside. The piping will be sandwiched between the lining and the bag at the front and back. Stitch together, making a ¼-inch seam, again sewing as close to the piping as possible along the front and back. Fold the lining strip to the inside and slip-stitch securely in place all around.

For the straps, press or stitch the interfacing to the wrong side of each strip of fabric. With right sides together, stitch across one end and then down the long edge making a ¼-inch seam. Turn to the right side and press. Turn the raw edges inside and slip-stitch in place. Topstitch close to each edge. Slip-stitch the ends of the straps securely inside the tote bag just next to the seam of the first block.

Lattice

Fig. 86   Design.

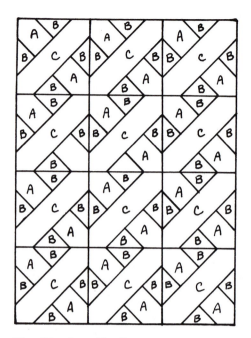

Fig. 87   Assembly diagram.

Easy
Pieces per side: 84 (168 total)
A   24 red, 24 green   C   12 red, 12 green
B   96 gold

The blocks are all made the same way, but with color changes to create the lattice effect. To make each block, sew a B to each side of A; then sew B-A-B to each side of C. Always sew the B-A-B triangles to a contrasting color C.

Outline-quilt each A and C piece by hand or machine using matching thread.

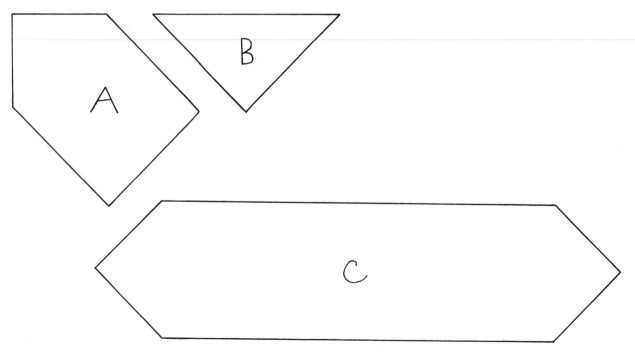

Fig. 88   Templates for Lattice.

Whirling Poinsettias

(Color page 77)

Fig. 89   Design.

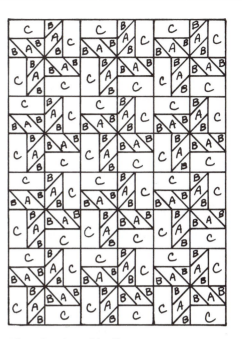

Fig. 90   Assembly diagram.

Moderate

Pieces per side: 192 (384 total)

A   24 white, 24 solid
     red, 24 medium
     red, 24 bright red

B   48 solid green,
     48 light green,
     48 medium green,
     48 bright green

C   24 solid green,
     24 light green,
     24 medium green,
     24 bright green

The square units within each block are all made the same way; the changes of fabric and color create visual excitement. To make each square unit, sew a B to each long edge of A; sew a C to B-A-B. Follow the diagram carefully to construct the other 3 squares of the first unit, then sew 2 pairs of squares together to make each half of the block. Sew the halves together to complete the design. Follow the assembly diagram very carefully for the changes of fabric and color.

Using red thread, outline-quilt each poinsettia by hand or machine.

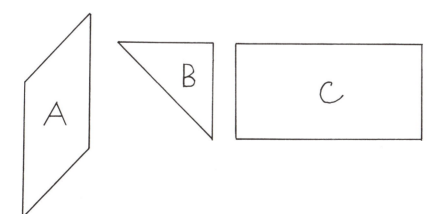

Fig. 91   Templates for Whirling Poinsettias.

POT HOLDERS

Brighten up your kitchen work area by making one or both of these useful pot holders. The patchwork and sewing are very quick and easy and a good way to use your scrap fabrics. Make them using the Quilt-as-You-Go Method.

Ball Pot Holder

(Color page 75)

Fig. 92   Design.

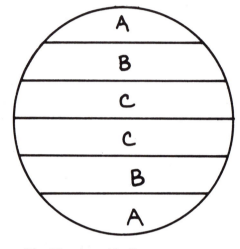

Fig. 93   Assembly diagram.

Easy
Finished Size: 6" diameter
Requirements
Round design: 1   6" diameter—scrap
Back (circle): 6½" diameter—scrap
Batting (circle): 1   6" diameter
Binding*: 1   1" × 20"—bias scrap
Loop: 1   1" × 4"—scrap
*As the binding must be cut on the bias, it would be far easier to use purchased double-fold bias tape.
Pieces per design: 6
A   2 bright   *C   1 light, 1 dark*
B   2 medium

Prepare the back and batting, following instructions for the Quilt-as-You-Go Method. Baste the dark C, right side up, to the batting so the long edge is ¼

inch above the middle of the circle. Stitch the long edges of the light and dark C's with right sides together and raw edges even. Fold the light C to the right side and finger-press in place. Sew B to each C in the same manner; then sew A to each B to complete the design.

If using bias-cut fabric, prepare the binding; see Binding a Project. If using bias tape, unfold one long edge of the 20-inch strip. Pin the binding to the right side of the pot holder with raw edges even. Fold under one end and overlap with the other to conceal the raw edges. Stitch all around ¼ inch from the edges. Turn the binding over to the back and slip-stitch in place. Make the loop; see Loops & Ties. Slip-stitch the ends to the back of the pot holder.

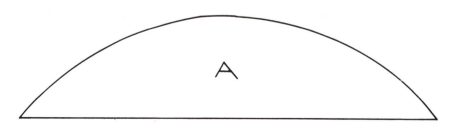

Fig. 94   Templates for Ball Pot Holder; continued on page 39.

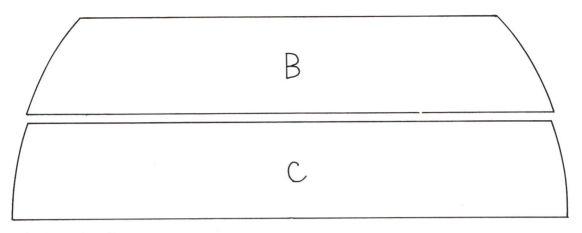

(Fig. 94 continued.)

Log Cabin Pot Holder

(Color page 75)

Fig. 95   Design.

Fig. 96   Assembly diagram.

Easy
Finished size: 7" square
Requirements
Block: 1   7" square—scraps of light and dark fabrics
Back: 1   7½" square—scrap
Batting: 1   7" square
Binding*: 3   1" × 7½"
*   1   1" × 10"*} —scrap
*If desired, use purchased double-fold bias tape for the binding.
Pieces per block: 13

A	*1 red, 1 light*	*E*	*1 light, 1 dark*
B	*1 light, 1 dark*	*F*	*1 light, 1 dark*
C	*1 light, 1 dark*	*G*	*1 dark*
D	*1 light, 1 dark*		

Prepare the back and batting, following instructions for the Quilt-as-You-Go Method. Baste red A in the upper left corner as shown in the assembly diagram. Stitch light A to red A. Stitch dark B to A-A with right sides together and raw edges even. Stitch light B to A-B in the same manner. Continue, following the assembly diagram, until the block is completed. Trim the back even with the top.

Prepare the binding fabric and bind the sides and bottom of the pot holder; see Binding a Project. For the top, pin the long strip in place with the extension at the red A corner; leave ¼ inch for turning at the opposite corner. Stitch as for the sides and bottom, finishing the corner. To make the loop, fold the remaining long raw edge of the extension ¼ inch to the wrong side to meet the central crease; fold the short end ¼ inch to the inside. Fold the strip in half and topstitch the edges together. Slip-stitch the end of the extension to the back of the pot holder for the loop.

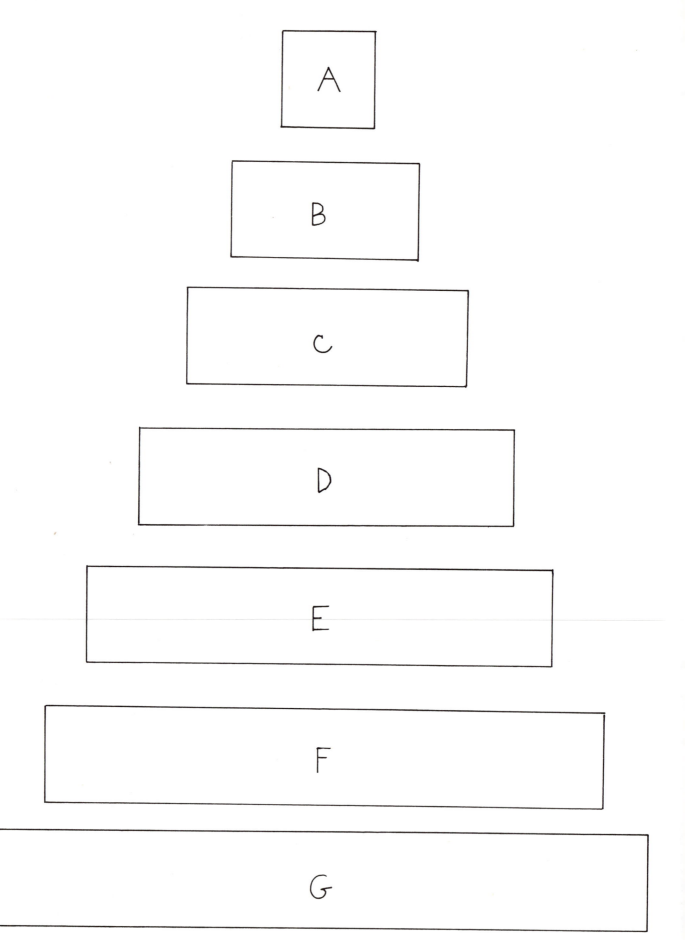

Fig. 97   Templates for Log Cabin Pot Holder.

Tree Place Mats & Napkins

(Color page 75)

Fig. 98 Design.

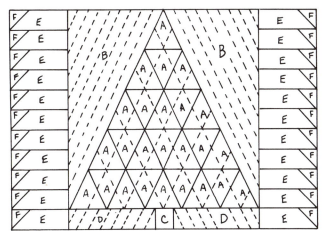

Fig. 99 Assembly diagram.

Easy

Finished size: 11½″ × 16½″

Requirements *(for 4 place mats and napkins)*

Pieced design: 4   11½″ × 16½″—¼ yard each of 4 greens; ⅜ yard dark green; scrap brown

Back: 4   13″ × 18″—1¼ yards red (includes fabric for B and D pieces)

Batting: 4   11½″ × 16½″

Binding: self-binding

Napkins: 4   15½″ × 15½″—⅞ yard matching fabric

Pieces per place mat: 74

A	4 white, 6 light green, 5 bright green, 5 medium green, 5 dark green	C	1 brown
		D	2 red
		E	11 dark green, 11 dark green reversed
B	1 red, 1 red reversed	F	22 white

Distinctive and appealing, these place mats and napkins will enhance your Christmas table. Use lovely traditional fabrics of red and green to lend quiet elegance to your holiday meals.

To make the place mat, first assemble the central tree rectangle; then construct the side strips and sew to each side of the rectangle.

Sew the A triangles together in rows, as shown in the assembly diagram. Sew the rows together to construct the tree. Sew a B to each side of the tree. Sew a D to each side of C; then sew D-C-D to the base of the tree to complete the central tree rectangle.

To make each side strip, sew an E to each F. Sew the matching E-F strips together in 2 groups with 11 strips in each group. Sew the pieced strips to each side of the central tree rectangle to complete the design.

See instructions under Assembling a Project for Quilting. Outline-quilt each E piece. Quilt the central tree rectangle following the assembly diagram. Self-bind each of the place mats as directed in Binding a Project.

To make the napkins, press the raw edges of the fabric squares ¼ inch to the wrong side and repeat to enclose the raw edges. Topstitch close to the inner pressed edge.

Fig. 100   Templates for Tree Place Mats & Napkins; continued on page 41.

41

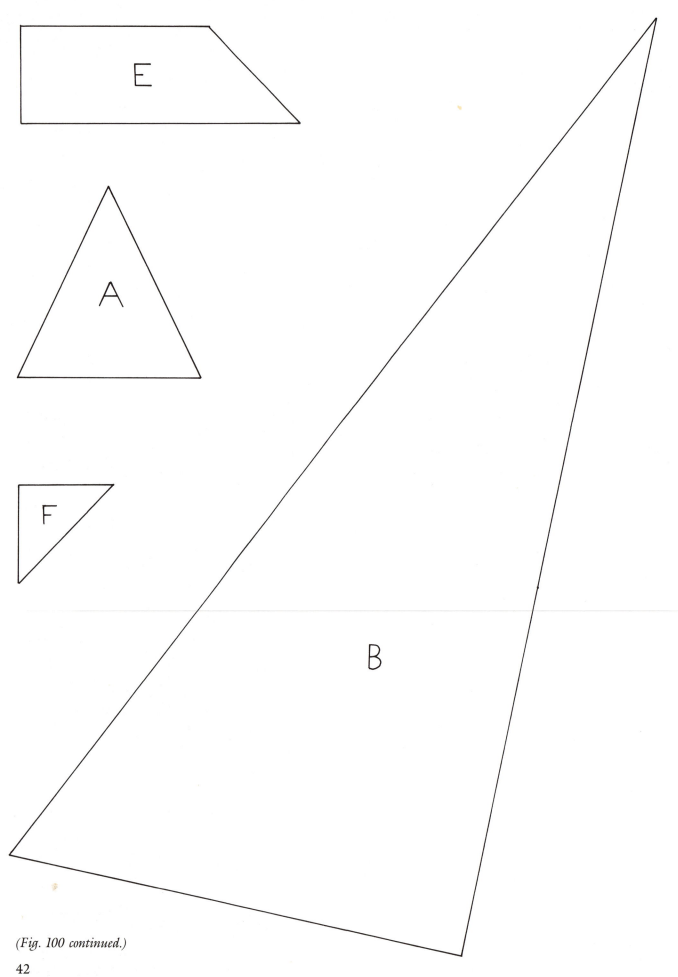

(Fig. 100 continued.)

42

Block Designs: 12 Inches Square

Home for the Holidays

(Color page 80)

Fig. 101   Design.

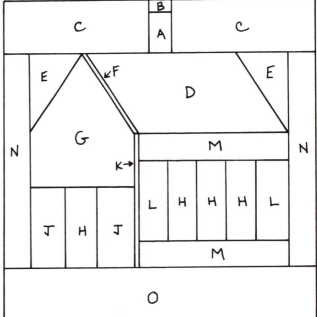

Fig. 102   Assembly diagram.

Moderate
Pieces per block: 23

A	1 bright	J	2 bright
B	1 light	K	1 light
C	2 sky	L	2 bright
D	1 dark	M	2 bright
E	1 sky, 1 sky reversed	N	2 sky
F	1 light	O	1 medium
G	1 bright		
H	1 light, 2 yellow, 1 bright		

Piece this delightful house design in colors to match your own home. Make the sky in a white polka dot on blue fabric to represent falling snow. If you're an adept embroiderer, you can plan to add homey touches such as a wreath, your house number, and a doorknob to create a very personalized design.

To begin, sew A to B; then sew C to each side of A-B. Sew an E to the right edge of D and F to the left edge. Sew the remaining E to the upper left edge of G. Sew the upper right edge of G to F.

Next, sew a J to each side of light H. Sew J-H-J to G. For the windows and side of the house, sew a bright H between the 2 yellow H's; sew an L to each end. Sew M to the top and bottom of the strip just made. Sew K to the left edge of M-L-M. Inset the side of the house into the roof and front; see How to Inset. Sew an N to each side of the house. Sew C-A-C to the top and O to the bottom to complete the design.

For finishing touches, embroider a green wreath

in satin stitch on the front door using 3 strands of embroidery thread in the needle. Add red French knots for the berries. Embroider a large black French knot for the doorknob. Add other details, as desired.

Outline-quilt the house, windows, door, roof, and chimney.

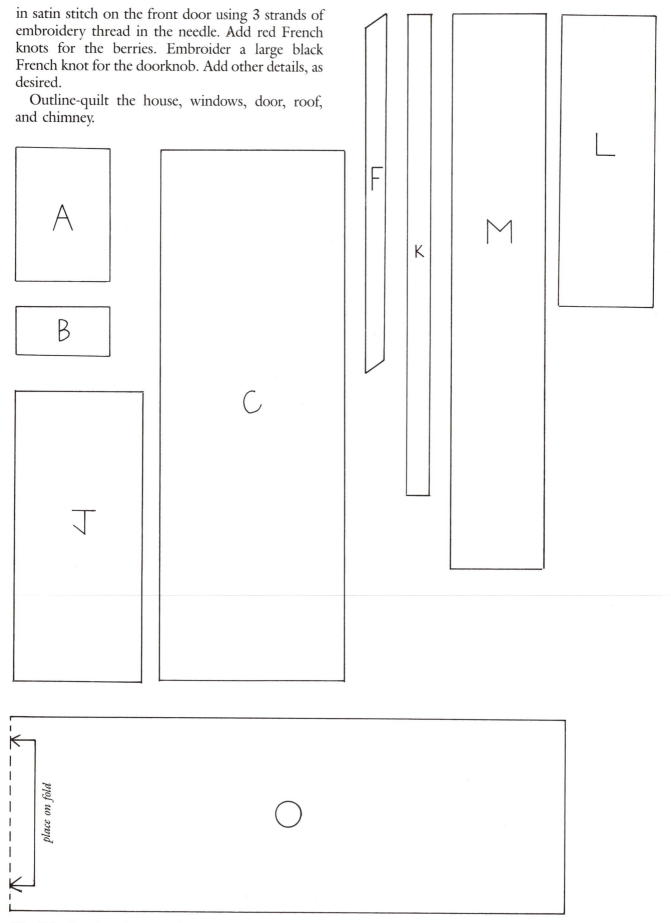

Fig. 103 *Templates for Home for the Holidays; continued on page 45.*

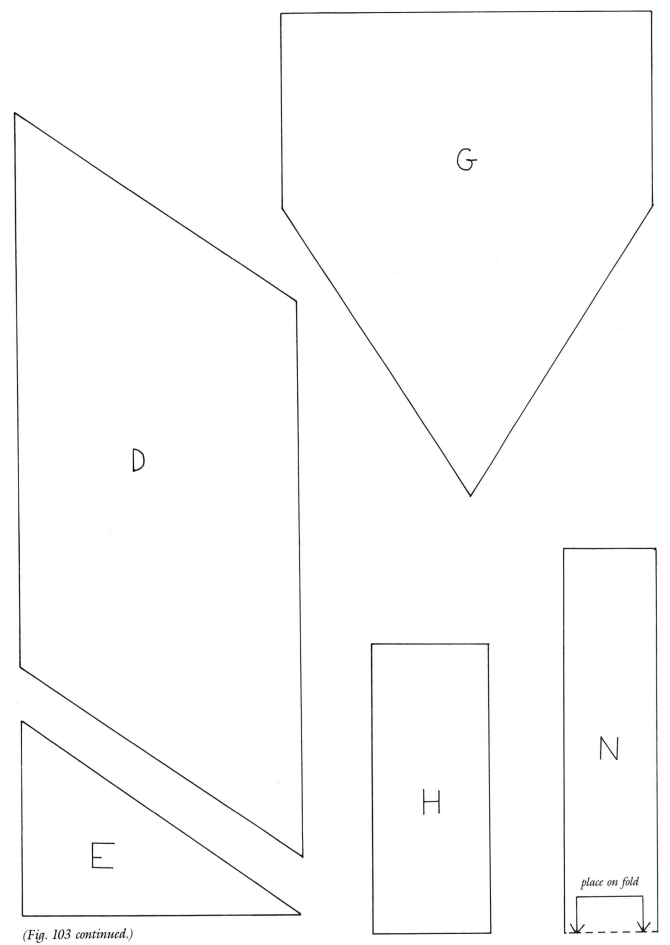

G

D

E

H

N

place on fold

(Fig. 103 continued.)

45

Holly Wreath

(Color page 80)

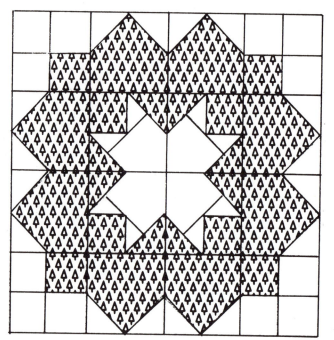

Fig. 104   Design.

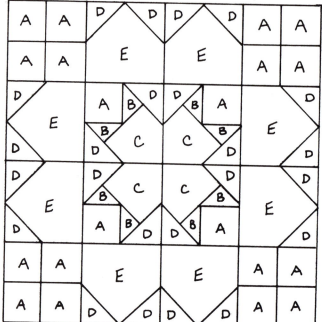

Fig. 105   Assembly diagram.

Easy
Pieces per block: 64

A	12 light, 8 bright	D	16 light, 8 bright
B	8 light	E	8 bright
C	4 light		

Wreaths are signs of welcome and cheer at Christmastime and this wreath is no exception; it will brighten any Christmas project you make.

Arrange all the pieces on a flat surface; then separate them into 4 rows, using the diagram as a guide.

For the central squares, sew 2 B's to adjacent edges of A. Sew C to B-B; then sew D to each B-C edge.

For the corner squares, sew 2 pairs of A pieces together; then join the pairs to make each square.

For the side squares, sew a D to each angled edge of E.

Sew the squares in rows with 4 squares in each row. Matching seams carefully, sew the rows together to complete the design.

If you are using a solid green fabric for the wreath, embroider French knots at random all over the wreath, to resemble berries using 6 strands of red thread in the needle.

Outline-quilt the inner and outer edges of the wreath; then add a row of quilting ½ inch from the inner and outer edges of the wreath.

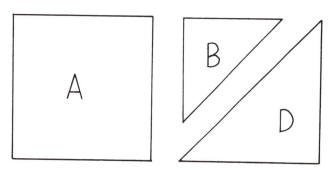

Fig. 106   Templates for Holly Wreath.

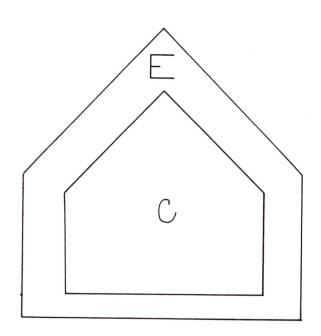

Christmas Star

(Color page 80)

Fig. 107   Design.

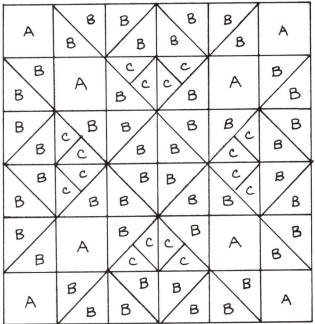

Fig. 108   Assembly diagram.

Easy
Pieces per block: 72
A   *4 bright, 4 dark*
B   *8 light, 24*
     medium, 16 dark
C   *8 light, 8 dark*

Stars are popular Christmas symbols, and this time-honored version is always a favorite. Careful matching of seams is essential. So take your time, press well and use lots of pins while piecing, for perfect results.

Arrange all the cut pieces on a flat surface as shown in the diagram. First, sew together all the B-B squares. Next, sew together the C pieces; then sew C-C's to each remaining B, making 8 B-C squares.

Sew all the squares together in 6 rows, with 6 squares in each row. Finally, sew the rows together to complete the design.

Quilt the inner and outer edges of the central star and the medium B pieces in each corner. Outline-quilt the edges of the light B and C pieces to emphasize the background diamond.

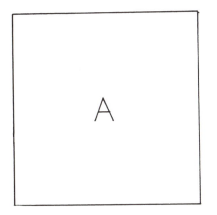

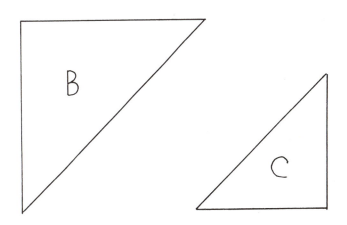

Fig. 109   Templates for Christmas Star.

Fireplace

(Color page 80)

Fig. 110 Design.

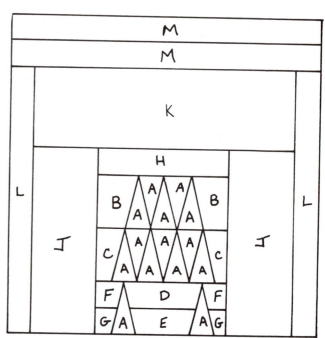

Fig. 111 Assembly diagram.

Easy
Pieces per block: 32

A	2 light, 10 assorted flame colors, 2 gold
B	1 light, 1 light reversed
C	1 light, 1 light reversed
D	1 brown
E	1 light
F	1 brown, 1 brown reversed
G	1 light, 1 light reversed
H	1 light
J	2 bright
K	1 bright
L	2 medium
M	1 light, 1 medium

Find fabrics that will make this design seem real—a brick fireplace, framed by an old-fashioned print for the wallpaper and brown logs burning with bright, fiery colors for the flames.

Arrange pieces A-H on a flat surface to choose the best possible mix of "flames." Sew the flames together in 2 horizontal strips with the B and C pieces at each outer edge. Use the gold A pieces for the grates; sew each F to G and D to E; then sew to the grates as shown. Sew the grate strip to the bottom of the flames; sew H to the top.

Next, sew J to each side of the pieced central portion. Sew K to the top; then sew L to each side. Sew the M's together; then sew the light M to L-K-L to complete the design.

Outline-quilt each flame, the log and grates; then quilt around the fireplace and mantle.

Fig. 112 Templates for Fireplace; *continued on page 49.*

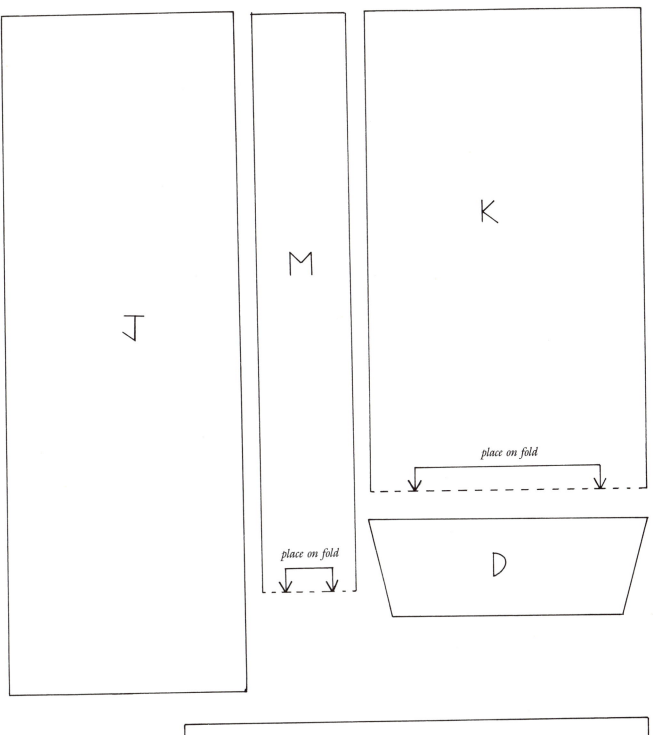

place on fold

place on fold

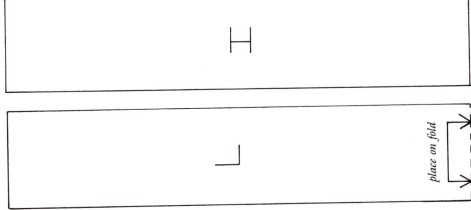

place on fold

(*Fig. 112 continued.*)

Cat

(Color page 79)

Fig. 113 Design.

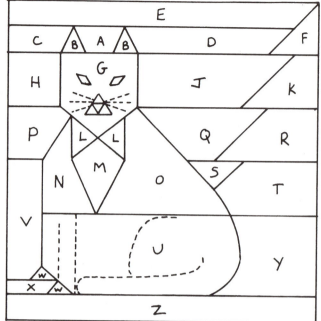

Fig. 114 Assembly diagram.

Challenging
Pieces per block: 28

A	1 bright	O	1 dark
B	2 dark	P	1 bright
C	1 bright	Q	1 bright
D	1 dark	R	1 medium
E	1 bright	S	1 bright
F	1 medium	T	1 medium
G	1 dark	U	1 dark
H	1 bright	V	1 bright
J	1 bright	W	2 light
K	1 medium	X	1 bright
L	2 accent colors	Y	1 bright
M	1 light	Z	1 bright
N	1 dark		

This is probably the most difficult design in the book, but certainly worth the effort. It is a portrait of our beloved Emily; change the body color to match your own cat.

Mark and cut the fabrics carefully; then take your time when sewing curves or insetting corners; see Sewing Curves and How to Inset.

For the ears strip, sew a B to each side of A. Sew C to the left B and D to the right B; then sew E to the top. Sew F to E-D.

For the face strip, sew H to the left side of G and J to the right side. Sew J to K; then sew the strip just made to the ears strip.

Next, construct the body. Sew the L pieces to the top of M. Inset L-M into N and O as shown in the diagram. Sew P to N. Next, sew Q to R and S to T; sew these 2 strips together; then sew to O, curving your stitches at the T end. Now, carefully sew U to Y, easing Y to fit. Sew U-Y to N-O-T. Sew one W to X and one W to V; sew V-W to X-W following the diagram. Inset N-U into V-W; then sew the top of V to P. Sew Z to the base of the cat; then inset the face strip to the body to complete the design, taking special care where the chin touches the bow tie.

Transfer the embroidery markings to the face. Using 6 strands of gold embroidery floss in the needle and satin stitch, embroider the eyes; add one long straight stitch with 4 strands of black down the middle of each eye for the pupil. Using 6 strands of white floss in the needle, embroider the nose in satin stitch and the whiskers in outline stitch.

To delineate the legs and tail, transfer the quilting markings from the pattern to the U piece using tailor's chalk. Quilt by hand or machine, or embroider in outline stitch.

Using matching thread, quilt around the cat's body, bib, feet, and bow tie; then quilt along the branches of the tree.

Fig. 115 *Templates for Cat; continued on pages 52 and 53.*

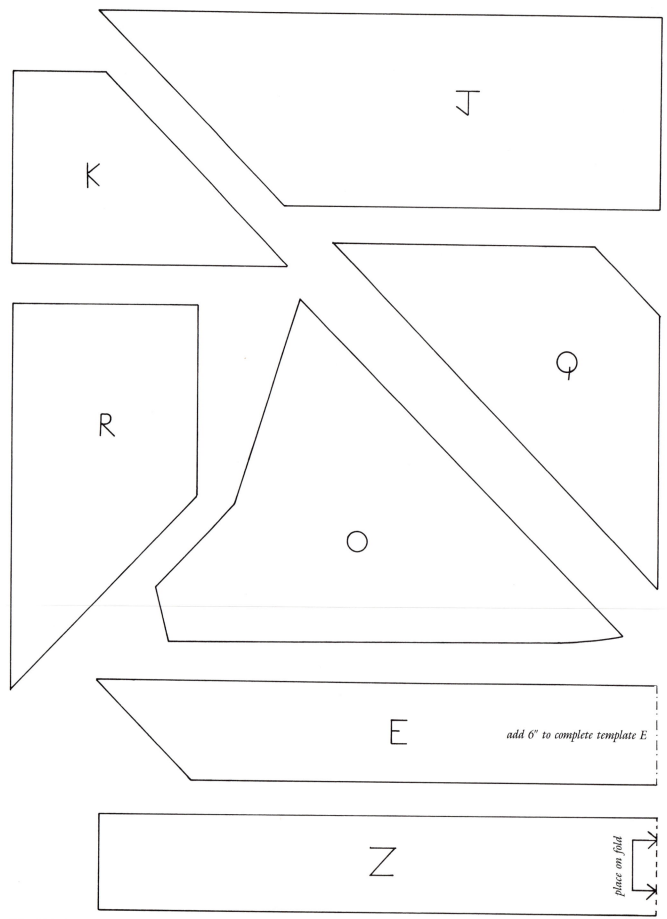

add 6" to complete template E

place on fold

(Fig. 115 continued.)

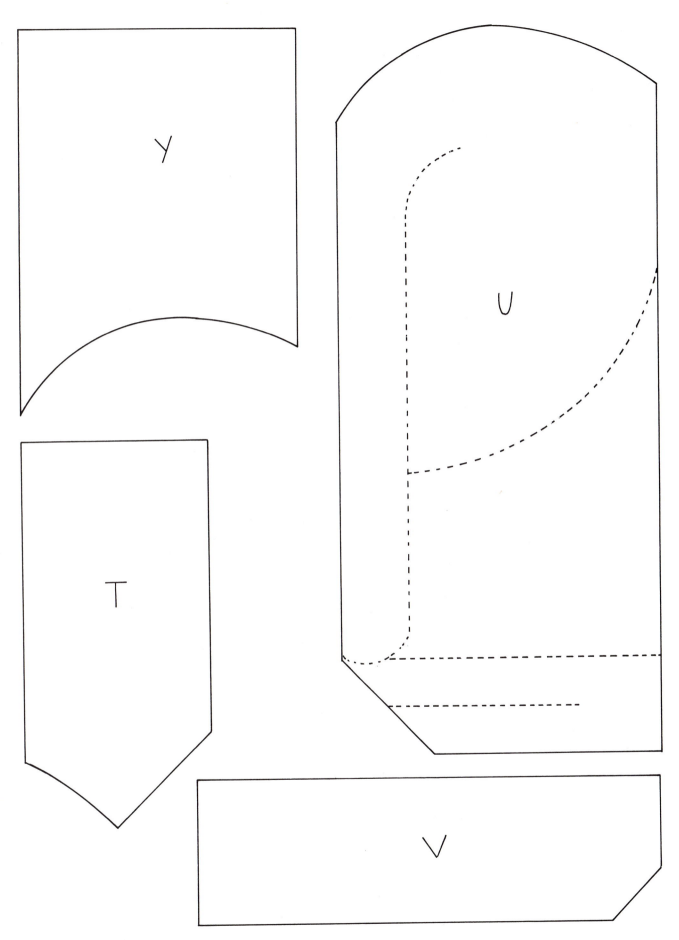

(Fig. 115 continued.)

53

Dog

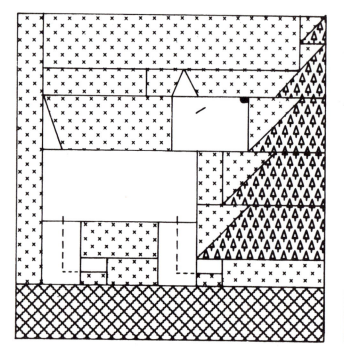

Fig. 116 Design.

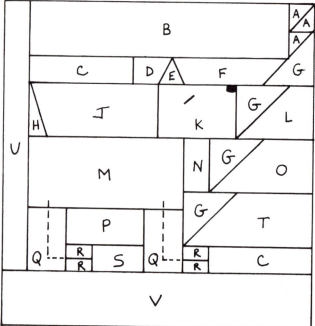

Fig. 117 Assembly diagram.

Easy

Pieces per block: 31

A	2 bright, 1 medium	L	1 medium
B	1 bright	M	1 light
C	2 bright	N	1 bright
D	1 bright	O	1 medium
E	1 light	P	1 bright
F	1 bright	Q	2 light
G	3 bright, 1 medium	R	2 light, 2 bright
		S	1 bright
H	1 light	T	1 medium
J	1 bright	U	1 bright
K	1 light	V	1 bright

Dog lovers of all ages will be proud to display this handsome fellow at Christmas or any time. You'll only need to add simple embroidery for the face and legs; appliqué a collar to the neck for a festive touch, if you like; see How to Appliqué.

To begin, arrange the 3 A's as shown in the diagram; sew together, creating a straight edge with the bright A patches; sew B to A-A. For the ear strip, sew C to D, D to E, and E to F; sew to the A-B strip. Sew medium G to the angled edge of the patchwork just made.

Next, construct the rest of the body and tree: Sew H to J and J to K. Sew G to L; then sew G to K. Sew this strip to the ear strip. For the feet, sew each light R to a bright R; sew one foot to S and the other to the remaining C. Sew R-S to P; then sew Q to each side of the rectangle just made. Sew Q-P-Q to M. Sew N to G and G to O. Sew the remaining G to T; then join to the N-G-O strip. Sew R-C to the other edge of the G-T strip. Sew N-G-R to M-Q; then attach to the top of the block.

Sew U to the left edge of the block. Sew V to the base to complete the design.

If desired, cut a ⅞- × 1½-inch piece of fabric for the collar; press all raw edges ¼" to the wrong side. Appliqué, slightly angled, to the dog's neck.

For the face, using 6 strands of black cotton floss in the needle, embroider a nose with satin stitch and an eye with straight stitch. Using one strand of black floss, delineate the front and back legs with outline stitch.

Outline-quilt the dog, tree and carpet. Quilt along the outline stitch delineating the front and back legs.

54

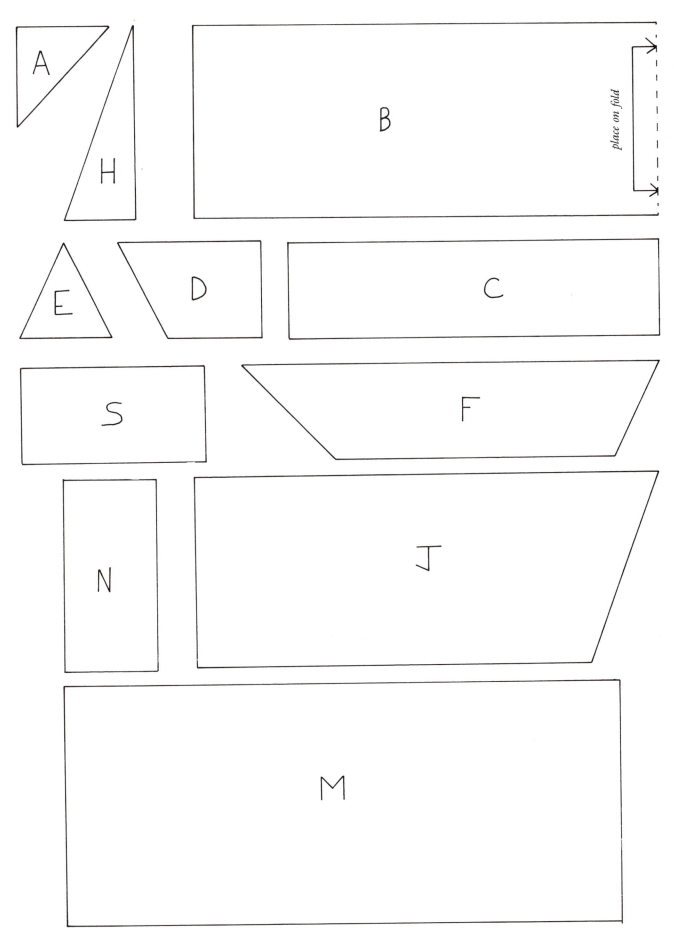

Fig. 118   Templates for Dog; continued on page 56.

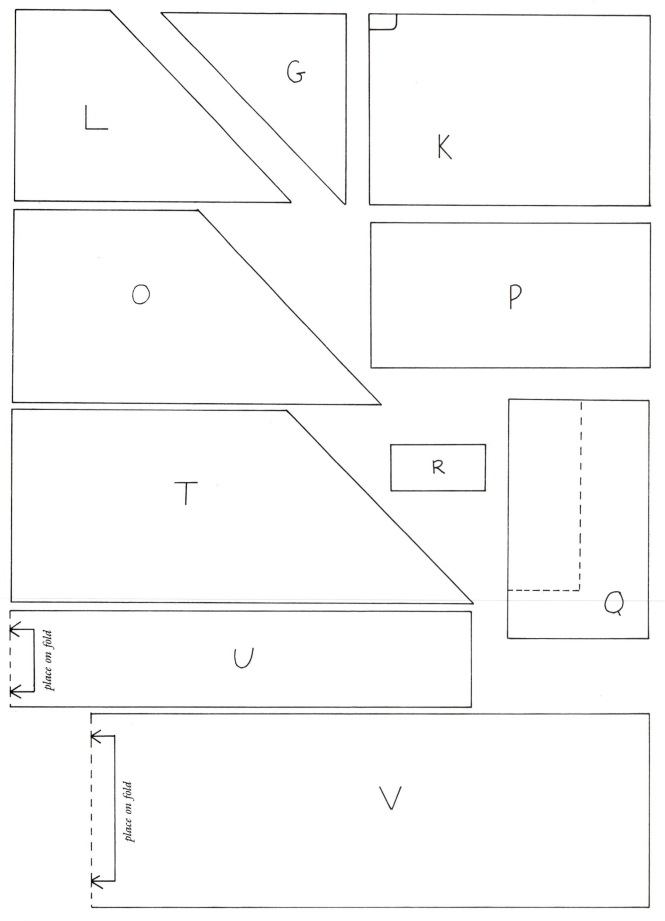

Letters on templates: L, G, K, O, P, T, R, Q, U, V

place on fold

place on fold

(Fig. 118 continued.)

56

Yuletide Cheer

(Color page 69)

Fig. 119   Design.

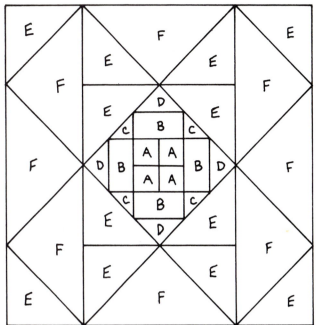

Fig. 120   Assembly diagram.

Easy
Pieces per block: 36

A	2 light, 2 dark	D	4 light
B	4 medium	E	4 bright, 8 dark
C	4 light	F	4 bright, 4 dark

For a lovely three-dimensional effect, use a striped fabric at right angles for the E and F patches as shown in the diagram. The block consists of 2 large triangles sewn to each side of a central diagonal patchwork strip.

Assemble the diagonal strip first: Sew the 4 A's together, alternating colors as shown in the diagram. Sew a B to the top and bottom of the A square. Sew a C to each short end of the remaining B's; then sew to each side of the A square. Sew D to each B to make the central square.

Next, sew together 2 pairs of bright and dark E's; then sew each to a bright F. Sew a dark E to one side of each F following the diagram; then sew the E-F pentagons to each side of the central square.

For each triangle, sew 2 pairs of bright and dark E's together, and sew each to a bright F. Following

the diagram carefully, sew a dark E to the bright F; then sew a dark F to each side of the pentagons just made. Sew the triangles to each side of the central strip to complete the design.

Outline-quilt the light and bright pieces.

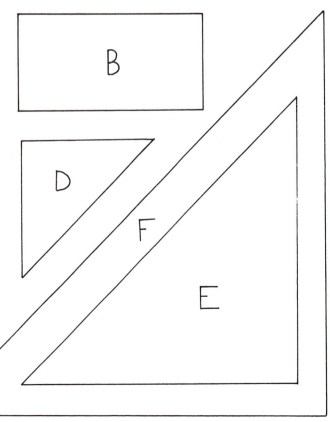

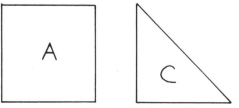

Fig. 121   Templates for Yuletide Cheer.

Basket of Poinsettias

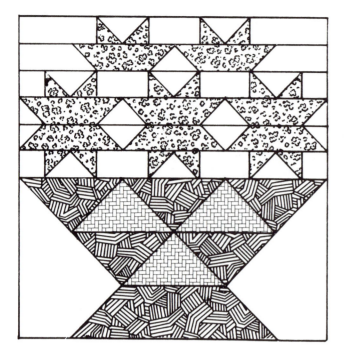

Fig. 122   Design.

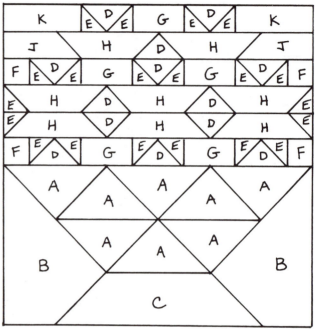

Fig. 123   Assembly diagram.

Moderate
Pieces per block: 65

A	3 medium, 5 dark	F	4 light
		G	5 light
B	1 light, 1 light reversed	H	8 bright
		J	1 light, 1 light reversed
C	1 dark		
D	13 light	K	2 light
E	4 light, 16 bright		

Don't be intimidated by the 65 pieces needed to make this design—it's all easy sewing. I promise, the finished square will be a showpiece! Feature the design in a sampler quilt or use it to make a pillow or writing caddy. It is simply assembled in halves, with the poinsettias created by joining 6 pieced strips.

First, assemble the basket half: Sew the A pieces into 2 horizontal strips as shown in the diagram. Sew the strips together, matching seams carefully. Sew a B to each side of the A section. Inset C into the base of A-B; see How to Inset.

Next, construct the poinsettia half: Arrange the pieces on a flat surface following the diagram. Sew each row in strips as shown. Sew the strips together, matching seams carefully, to create the flowers. Sew the flowers to the basket to complete the design.

Outline-quilt the basket and each flower.

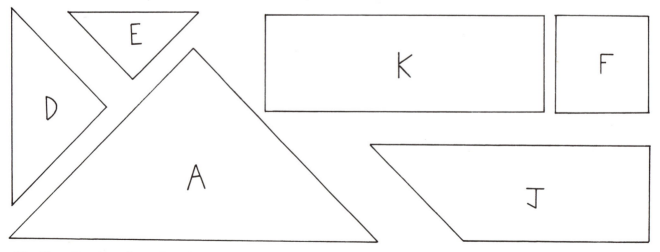

Fig. 124   Templates for Basket of Poinsettias; continued on page 60.

Christmas Tree

(Color page 80)

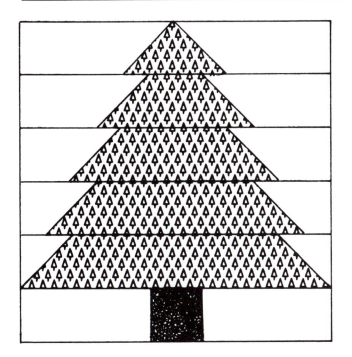

Fig. 125   Design.

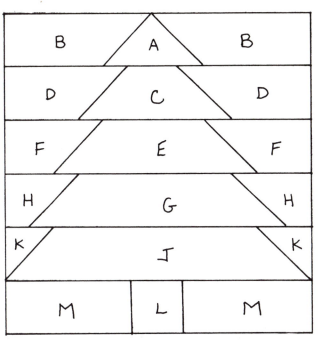

Fig. 126   Assembly diagram.

Easy
Pieces per block: 18

A	1 bright
B	1 light, 1 light reversed
C	1 bright
D	1 light, 1 light reversed
E	1 bright
F	1 light, 1 light reversed
G	1 bright
H	1 light, 1 light reversed
J	1 bright
K	2 light
L	1 dark
M	2 light

This simple yet dramatic design is very easily created in 6 patchwork strips with 3 pieces in each strip. For fun, embroider ornaments and garlands on the tree after you have sewn it.

Arrange the pieces on a flat surface following the diagram. Sew a light piece to each side of a bright or dark piece to assemble each strip. Sew the strips together to complete the design.

Outline-quilt each bright and dark piece; then add a row of quilting ½ inch outside the edges of the tree and trunk.

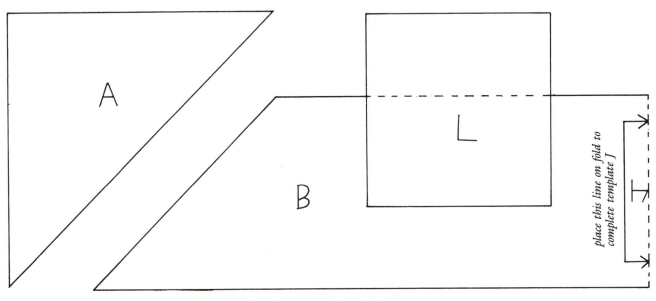

place this line on fold to complete template J

Fig. 127   Templates for Christmas Tree; continued on pages 60 and 63.

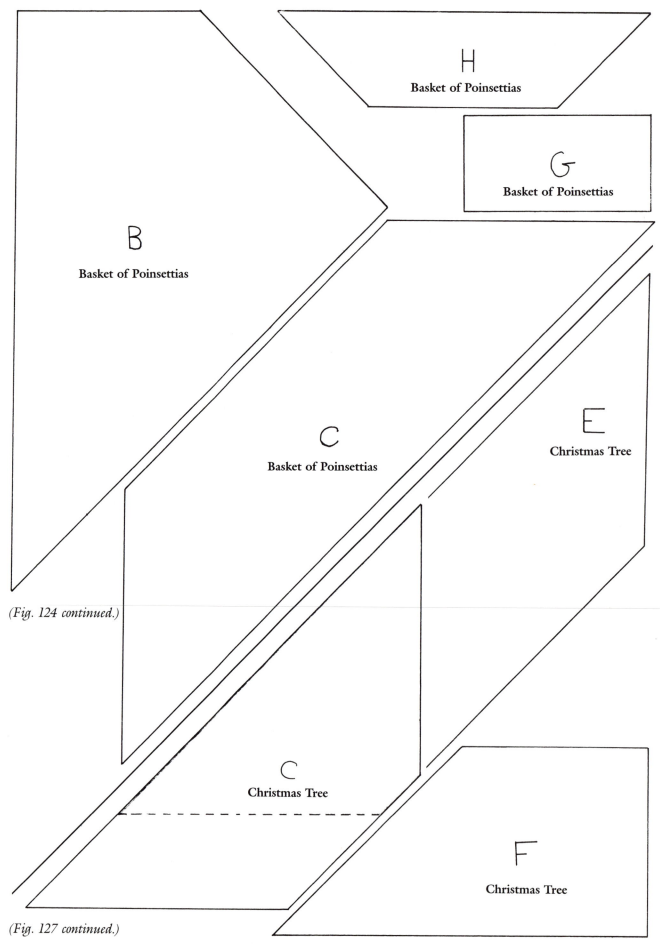

H
Basket of Poinsettias

G
Basket of Poinsettias

B
Basket of Poinsettias

C
Basket of Poinsettias

E
Christmas Tree

(Fig. 124 continued.)

C
Christmas Tree

F
Christmas Tree

(Fig. 127 continued.)

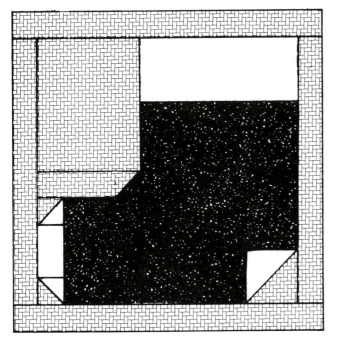

Fig. 128   Design.

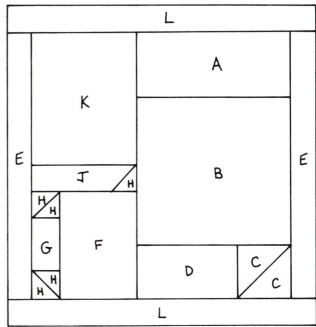

Fig. 129   Assembly diagram.

Easy
Pieces per block: 18

A	*1 light*	*G*	*1 light*
B	*1 bright*	*H*	*2 light, 1 bright,*
C	*1 light, 1 medium*		*2 medium*
D	*1 bright*	*J*	*1 medium*
E	*2 medium*	*K*	*1 medium*
F	*1 bright*	*L*	*2 medium*

Personalize this stocking by embroidering a name across it after completing the patchwork, but before quilting. This is an excellent yet subtle way to sign your own quilt; add the date for historical reference. If you are making this project as a gift, sign the recipient's name instead.

To begin, sew A to B. Sew the C's together to make a square; then sew the light C to D. Sew D-C to B. Sew E to the right edge of A-B-C.

For the toe, sew a light H to each medium H; then sew the light H's to each side of G. Sew H-G-H to F. Sew the remaining H to J. Sew J-H to H-F; then sew J to K. Sew E to the left edge of the patchwork just made.

Sew the toe section to the stocking. Sew L to the top and bottom of the pieced stocking to complete the design.

When ready to embroider, first practise writing the name on a scrap of paper the same size as piece B; then lightly pencil the name onto the fabric. Use outline stitch in a contrasting color, with 6 strands of cotton floss or a single strand of pearl cotton in your needle. Add the date, if you wish.

Outline-quilt the outer edges of the stocking; then delineate the toe, heel, and stocking top with quilting. Add 2 or 3 more lines of quilting, each 3/8 inch apart, to echo the outline of the stocking.

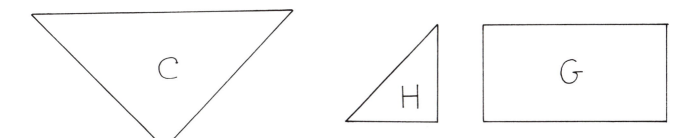

Fig. 130   Templates for Stocking; continued on pages 62 and 63.

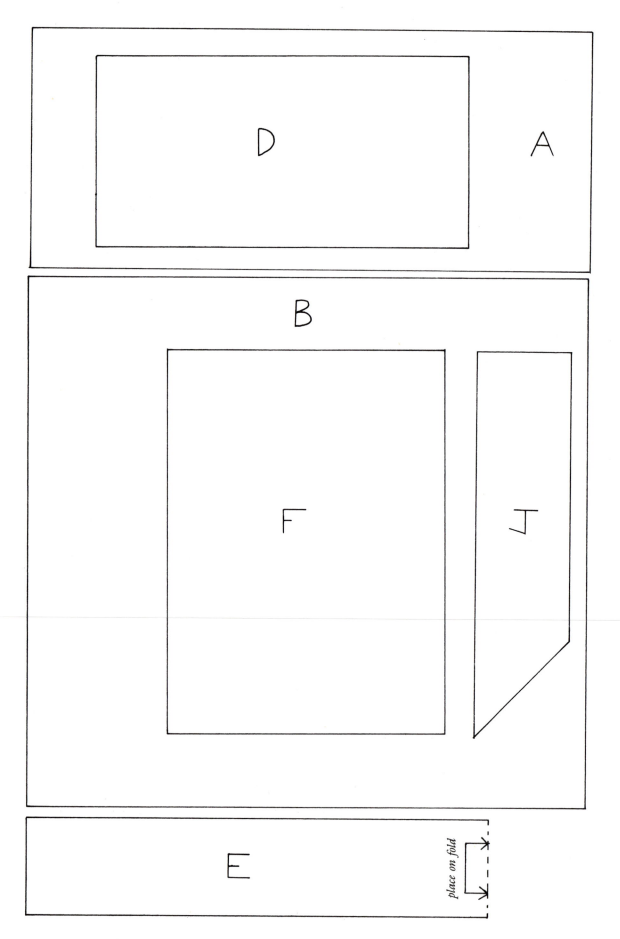

place on fold

(*Fig. 130 continued.*)

62

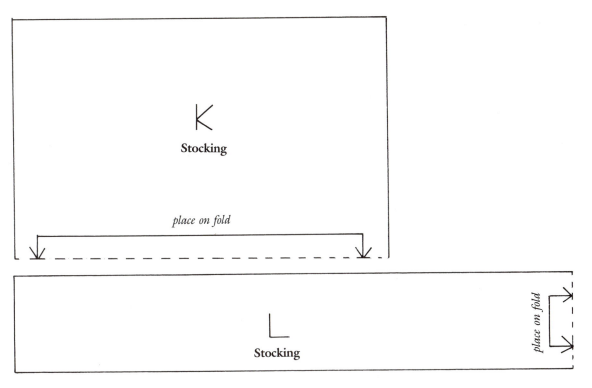

(Fig. 130 continued.)

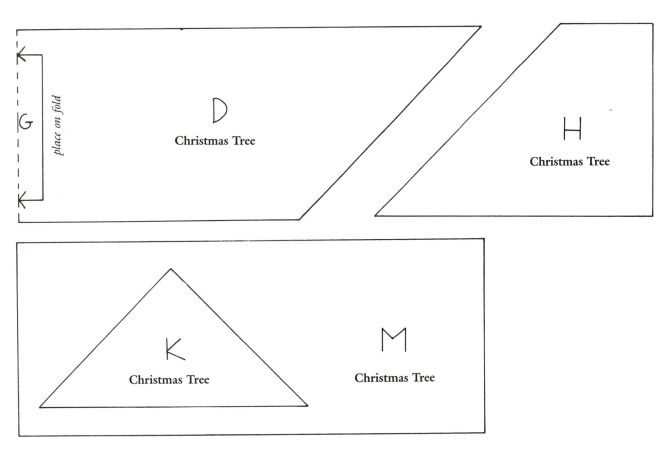

(Fig. 127 continued.)

Bow

Fig. 131 Design.

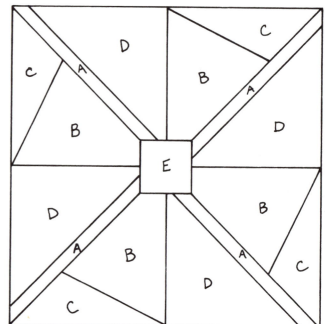

Fig. 132 Assembly diagram.

Easy or Challenging
Pieces per block: 17

A 4 medium
B 4 dark
C 4 light
D 4 light
E 1 dark

Use a striped fabric for the A pieces to emphasize the ribbon effect. There is an easy way (with appliqué) to make this design; the challenging method requires mitring.

Easy: Study the design; you'll see it is composed of 4 squares (each with a corner removed) joined in the middle with E. Make each square as follows: Sew B to C; then sew A to the B-C edge. Sew D to the opposite side of A. Sew each D to a B, joining the 4 squares with an opening in the middle. Appliqué E over the opening; see How to Appliqué.

Challenging: Sew B to C; then sew D to the B edge. Sew A to D. Repeat to make 3 more triangular shapes. Sew the A-D-B edge of each shape to E; then mitre A to B-C; see How to Mitre Corners.

Outline-quilt the ribbon and bow pieces.

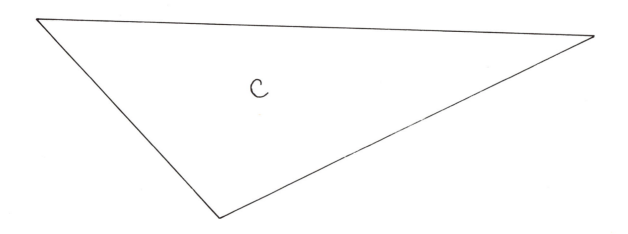

Fig. 133 Templates for Christmas Bow; continued on page 82.

A selection of Christmas Tree Ornaments (page 24).

Amish Shadowed Square (page 27).

A Nine-Patch Ornament (page 25) featuring teddy bears.

Antique toys brighten this Nine-Patch Ornament.

This Nine-Patch Ornament spotlights forest animals.

66

Variable Star (page 26).

Twinkling Star (page 26).

Shining Star (left, page 28); Wreath (right, page 28).

String Tree (left, page 29); Bow (right, page 28).

67

The blocks of the Christmas Table Runner, shown in detail on this page, are (clockwise, beginning at top left) Ribbons & Bows (page 81), Peace on Earth (page 114), and Yuletide Cheer (page 57). For a touch of whimsy, try Snowball Fight (page 96), Snowman (page 93), and Snowflake (page 92). To make a longer table runner, simply add more blocks; instructions are provided with the project.

(Opposite page)   Christmas Table Runner. Your holiday table will sparkle with good cheer when covered with a lovely table runner; select any of the 12-inch-square blocks (pages 43 to 115) for a unique creation.

A Christmas wreath is the most welcoming sight at Christmastime, hanging proudly on the front door. Patchwork Wreaths (page 21) are both simple and very quick to make. They will serve as excellent wall decorations during the holidays, too!
Star Wreath (top, page 22).
Ribbon Wreath (bottom, page 23).

(Opposite page) Decorations (page 120) make intriguing door and window displays—simply remove a few of the patchwork pieces to create a variety of shapes. Enhance the decoration by adding lace, ruffles, or piping. This example is Peace on Earth (page 114).

"I'll Be Home for Christmas" Wall Hanging (page 132). Anyone who's been in a faraway place at Christmastime can understand the longing for hearth and home during the holidays. This wall hanging celebrates those special feelings and at the same time allows you to show off your creativity and needlework skills.

Detail of "I'll Be Home for Christmas" Wall Hanging (page 132). A white eyelet fabric was chosen to simulate snow on the roof of the house, and a contrasting quilting thread was used to delineate the shingles. A Christmas tree is featured in one window, a cat in the other. Note the machine quilting on the trees; the roof, house, path, and field have been quilted by hand.

Writing Caddy (page 122). Any 12-inch-square block in this book can be used to make this project; the design shown here is Snow Crystal (page 91).

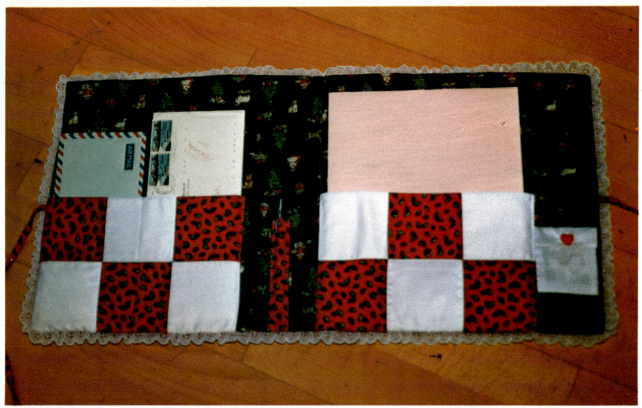

Writing Caddy open, shown with all the pockets.

Ball Pot Holder (page 38) and Log Cabin Pot Holder (page 39).

Chair Cushion (page 119); the design shown here is Christmas Eve (page 100).

Tree Place Mats & Napkins (page 41). This distinctive place mat and napkin set will enhance your Christmas fare.

The Argyle Stocking (page 31) is sure to inspire Santa to fill it with special gifts.

*Tote bags—Lattice (above left, page 36) and Whirling
Poinsettias (above right, page 37) will make Christmas
shopping easier for you.*

*House Doorstop (page 33). It's obvious that Scotty
approves of this Christmas decoration!*

Round Ruffled Pillow (page 118). This large pillow will provide a dramatic accent in any room of the house. The patchwork design shown is Dog (page 54).

Square Pillow with Lace & Ruffled Trim (page 118). This small pillow will fit easily on a child's chair or as part of a group of cushions. Guiding Star (page 109) is the patchwork design featured on the pillow front.

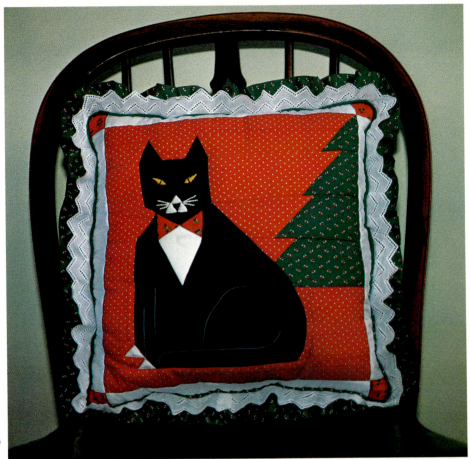

Square Pillow with Border & Ruffled Trim (page 117). This elaborate pillow design can be the showcase for a challenging patchwork pattern such as the Cat (page 50). Piping and lace have been added to demonstrate that each of the cushions can be as simple or fancy as you wish to make them.

Square Pillow with Border & Piping (page 117). Those who prefer simplicity will choose this type of pillow, which is certain to blend with every style of home decor. The patchwork pattern is Santa in Chimney (page 102).

This 16-Block Quilt (page 127) is a striking Sampler Quilt. Hung on the wall or displayed on a bed, the quilt will radiate the warmth and happiness of the holidays to all who see it.

Fig. 134   Design.

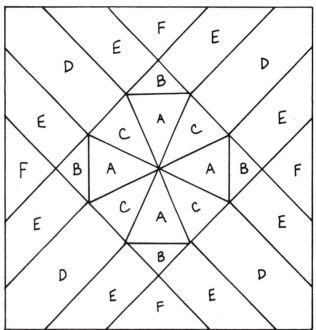

Fig. 135   Assembly diagram.

Easy
Pieces per block: 28

A	4 dark	E	4 light, 4 light
B	4 light		reversed
C	4 medium	F	4 dark
D	4 medium		

Pretty as a Christmas package, this design is composed of 2 triangles sewn to each side of a central diagonal strip. Try to find a vibrant striped fabric for the medium pieces and cut them as shown in the diagram and the color photo.

First, assemble the central bow: Sew a B to each

A. Sew each A-B to a C; then sew together 2 pairs of A-B-C pieces, forming each half of the bow. Press the central seams of each half in opposite directions to reduce bulk in the middle. Sew together the halves of the bow, matching the seams in the middle.

Next, sew an E to each side of each D. Sew E-D-E to opposite sides of the bow. Sew an F to each side of the remaining E-D-E pieces to form 2 large triangles. Sew a triangle to each side of the central diagonal strip to complete the design.

Outline-quilt the medium and dark pieces. If you are using a striped fabric, quilt along some of the stripes.

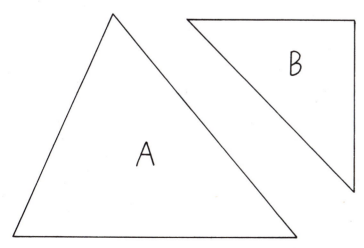

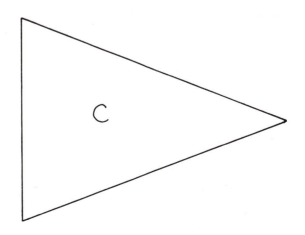

Fig. 136   Templates for Ribbons & Bows; continued on page 82.

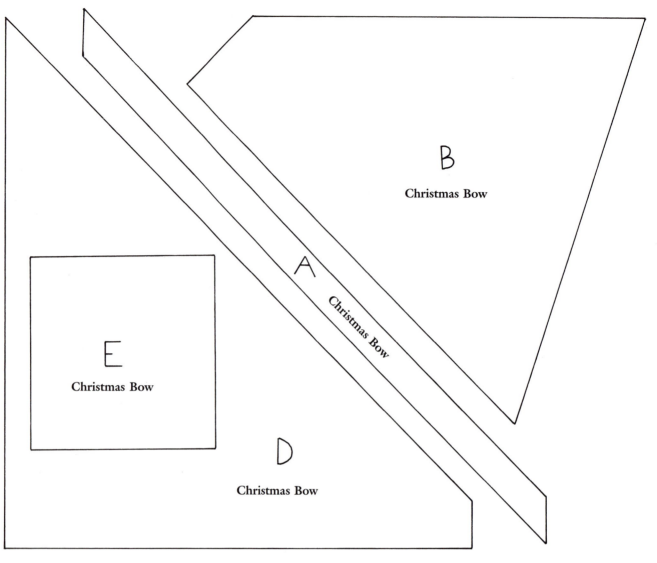

B
Christmas Bow

A
Christmas Bow

E
Christmas Bow

D
Christmas Bow

(Fig. 133 continued.)

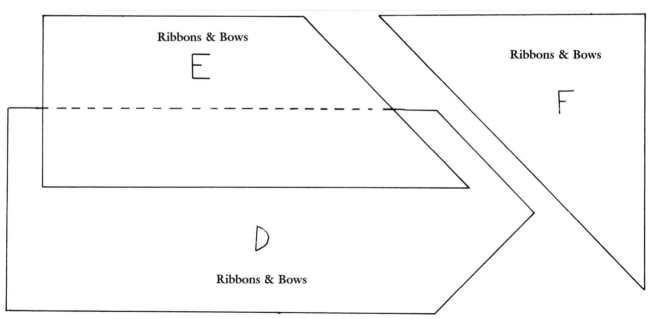

Ribbons & Bows
E

Ribbons & Bows
F

D
Ribbons & Bows

(Fig. 136 continued.)

Message Block

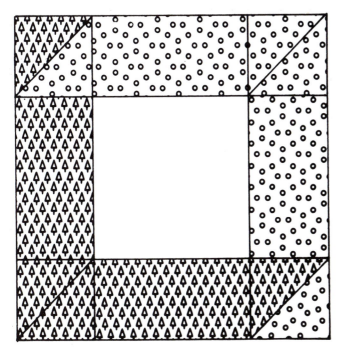

Fig. 137   Design.

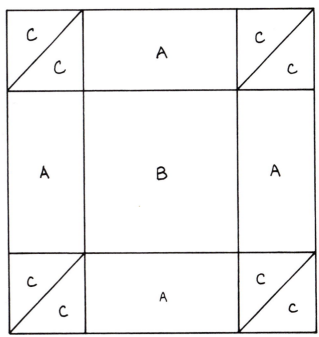

Fig. 138   Assembly diagram.

Easy
Pieces per block: 13
A   2 medium, 2 dark
B   1 light
C   4 medium, 4 dark

This simple design is especially appropriate at Christmastime when your own special message can be embroidered on the light patch. Or you can quilt a pretty motif in the central patch to celebrate the season. Here are some ideas you can use: the name of the gift's recipient; your name and the date; Noel; Merry Christmas (or Happy Christmas, for your English friends); Alleluia; Christmas and the year. Be sure to practise on a scrap of matching fabric to see the finished effect.

To begin, sew a medium and dark A to opposite sides of B. Sew 2 pairs of medium and dark C's together. Sew the remaining medium C's together to form 1 square; sew the remaining dark C's together to from another square. Sew the medium square to an end of medium A; sew the dark square to the other end of dark A. Sew the remaining squares to each A, matching the medium C to the medium A and the dark C to the dark A. Sew the strips just made to the top and bottom of A-B-A, as shown, to complete the design.

Outline-quilt the central square, the outer edges of the block, and the diagonal edges dividing each C square. If you are not writing or embroidering a message on the B patch, quilt a small flower, star, or bell in the middle.

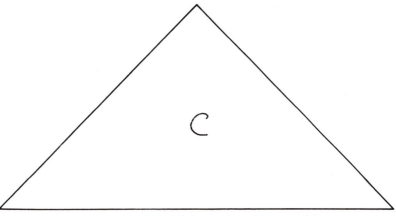

Fig. 139   Template for Message Block; continued on page 84.

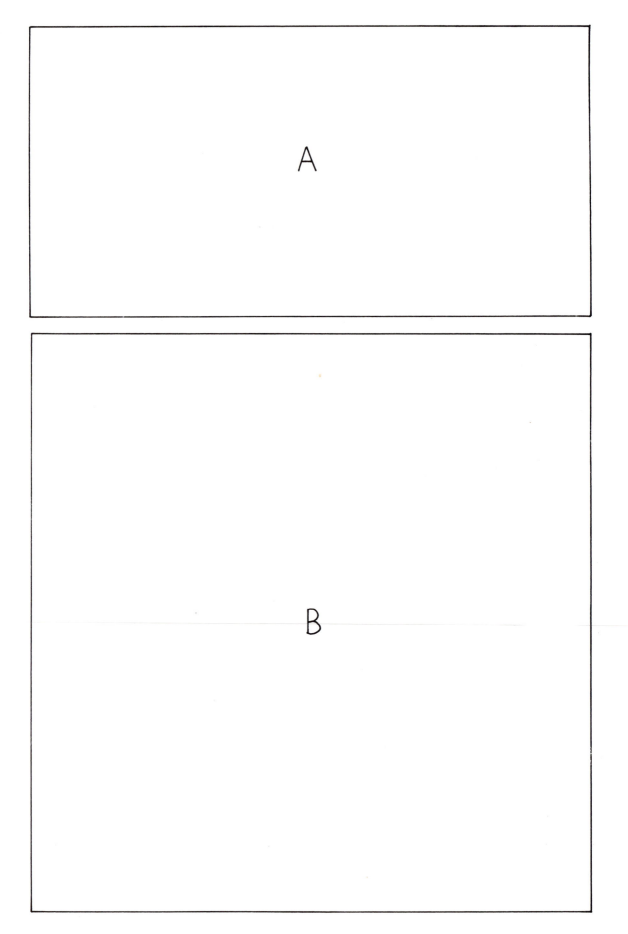

(Fig. 139 continued.)

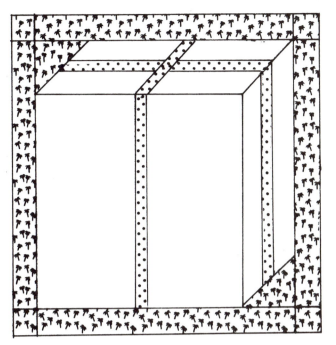

Fig. 140   Design.

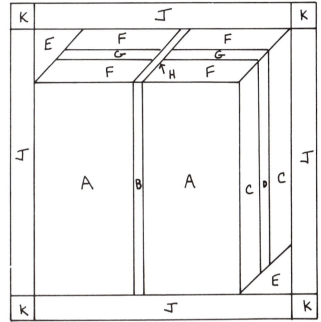

Fig. 141   Assembly diagram.

Moderate
Pieces per block: 23

A	2 light		F	4 light
B	1 bright		G	2 bright
C	2 light		H	1 bright
D	1 bright		J	4 medium
E	2 medium		K	4 medium

If you are making a project that will not receive much wear, add dimension to this design by making a real ribbon bow and sewing it where G crosses H. Insetting for this block is required only once; see How to Inset.

Sew an A to each side of B for the front of the gift. Sew a C to each long edge of D for the side; sew E to the bottom edge of C-D-C. Sew an F to each side of each G; sew F-G-F to each side of H for the top of the gift. Sew E to the left edge of F-G-F. Sew the top of the gift to the side, matching seams carefully. Inset the front into the top and sides.

Sew J to each side of the gift. Sew a K to each end of the 2 remaining J's; then sew to the top and bottom of the gift to complete the design.

Outline-quilt the edges of the gift and ribbon.

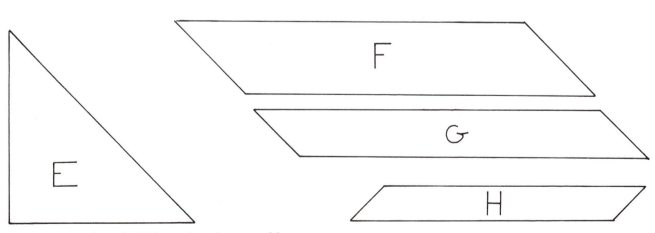

Fig. 142   Templates for Gift; *continued on page 86.*

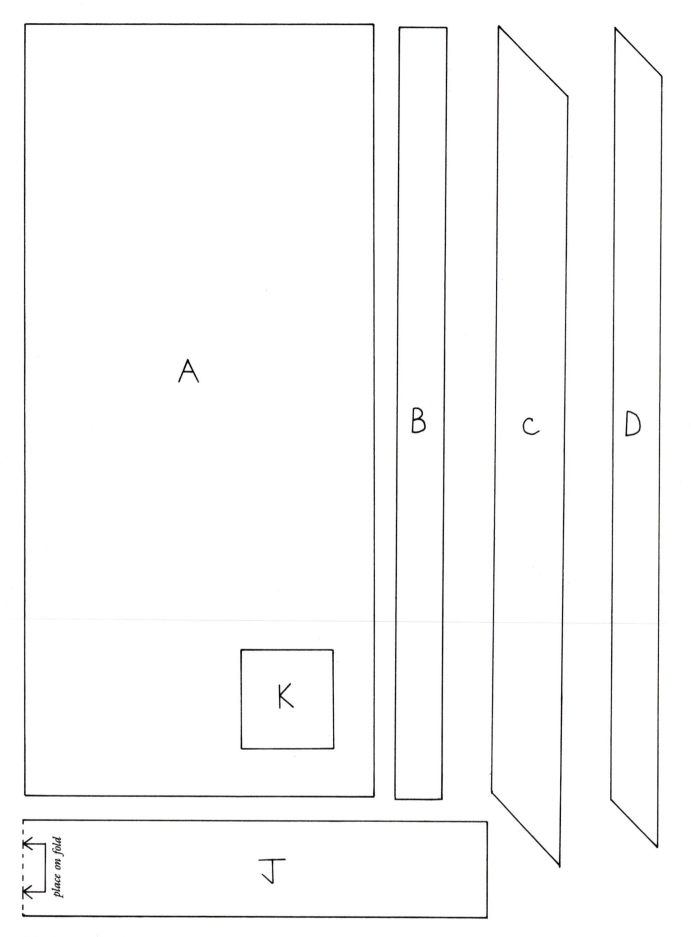

A

K

B

C

D

place on fold

J

(Fig. 142 continued.)

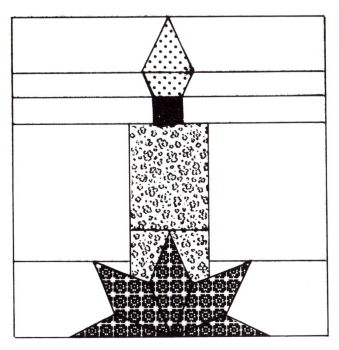

Fig. 143 Design.

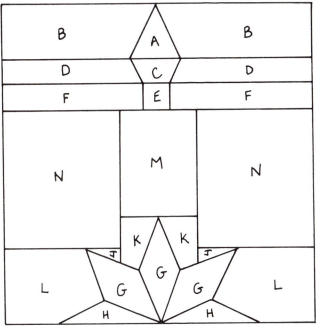

Fig. 144 Assembly diagram.

Challenging
Pieces per block: 23

A	1 gold	H	1 green, 1 green reversed
B	1 light, 1 light reversed	J	1 light, 1 light reversed
C	1 gold	K	1 bright, 1 bright reversed
D	1 light, 1 light reversed	L	1 light, 1 light reversed
E	1 dark		
F	2 light	M	1 bright
G	3 green	N	2 light

The bottom half of this design is quite difficult and should only be attempted by more experienced sewers; see How to Inset.

To begin, sew B to each side of A. Sew D to each side of C, and F to each side of E. Sew these 3 strips together for the flame and wick.

Next, sew the 3 G's together. Sew an H to each outer G, matching the dots. Following the diagram carefully, sew a J to each K, matching the diamonds; inset J-K between the G pieces. Inset L between each of the G-H pieces, matching the x's. Sew M to K-K; then inset N into each corner thus formed to complete the candle. Sew the flame and wick section to the candle to complete the design.

Outline-quilt the candle, flame, wick and each holly leaf. If desired, echo-quilt the central design across the background as shown in the color photograph.

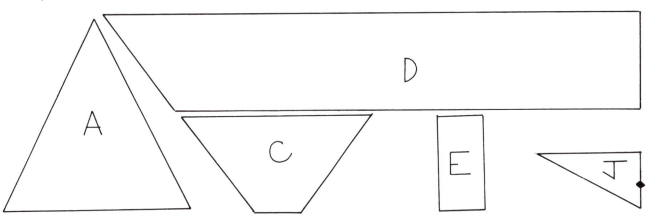

Fig. 145 Templates for Candle; continued on page 88.

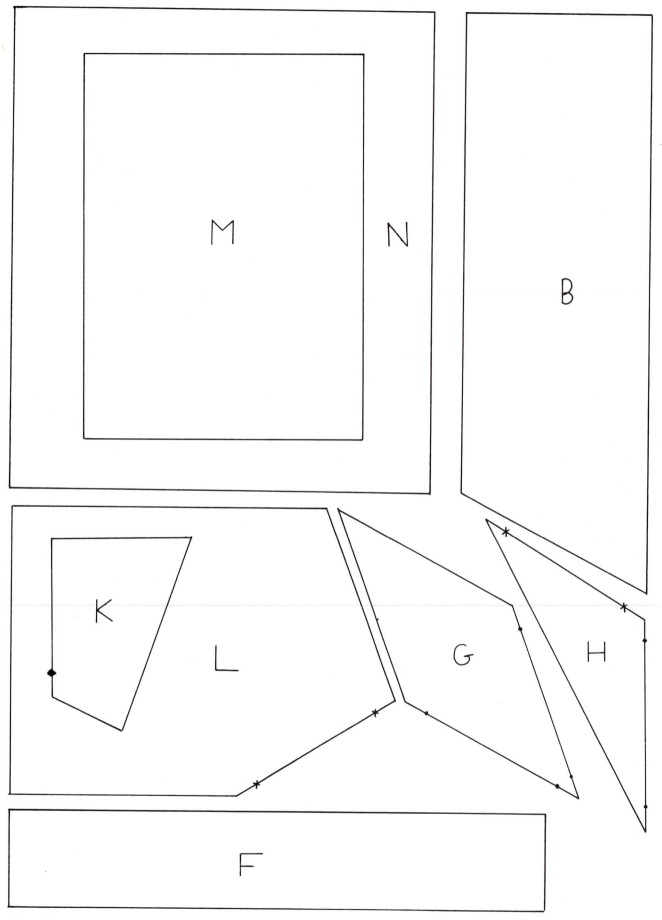

(Fig. 145 continued.)

Poinsettia Bouquet

Fig. 146 · Design.

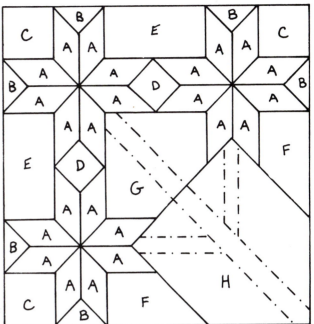

Fig. 147 Assembly diagram.

Challenging
Pieces per block: 41

A	12 bright, 12 bright reversed	E	2 light
B	6 light	F	1 light, 1 light reversed
C	3 light	G	1 light
D	2 light	H	1 light
		Stems	2 1" × 3¼"; 1" × 7½"

Elegant and distinctive, this design is a bit of a challenge to make because you'll be insetting a great deal; see How to Inset. To simplify the design, appliqué the stems (actually strips of fabric or bias tape) on the G and H pieces after the block has been pieced; see How to Appliqué.

First, make each of the 3 flowers: Sew each A piece to its reverse, forming 4 pairs of petals for each flower. Sew 2 of the pairs together, forming each half of the flower; press the central seams of each half in opposite directions to reduce bulk in the middle. Sew the halves of the flower together, matching the seam junction. Inset the B and C pieces between the petals on each flower, as shown in the diagram.

Join the flowers by insetting the D squares between the petals as shown. Next, inset the E and F pieces, following the diagram. Inset G in the central area; then inset H to complete the design.

For the stems, use bias tape; or cut your own tape and press each long edge of each fabric strip ¼ inch to the wrong side to make a ½-inch strip. First, pin the short stems to H between the dot-dash lines; appliqué in place, finishing off the edges near the flowers and leaving the edges near the central stem raw. Pin the long stem to G and H between the dot-dash lines, covering the raw edges of the short stems. Appliqué in place, finishing off the end near the flower. The other end can be left raw; trim that end to match the edge of the block.

Outline-quilt the poinsettias and the stems; then add a row of quilting ½ inch away from the first.

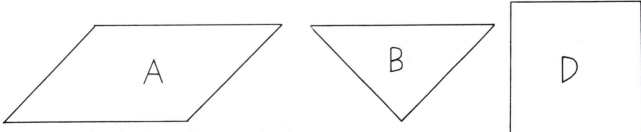

Fig. 148 Templates for Poinsettia Bouquet; continued on page 90.

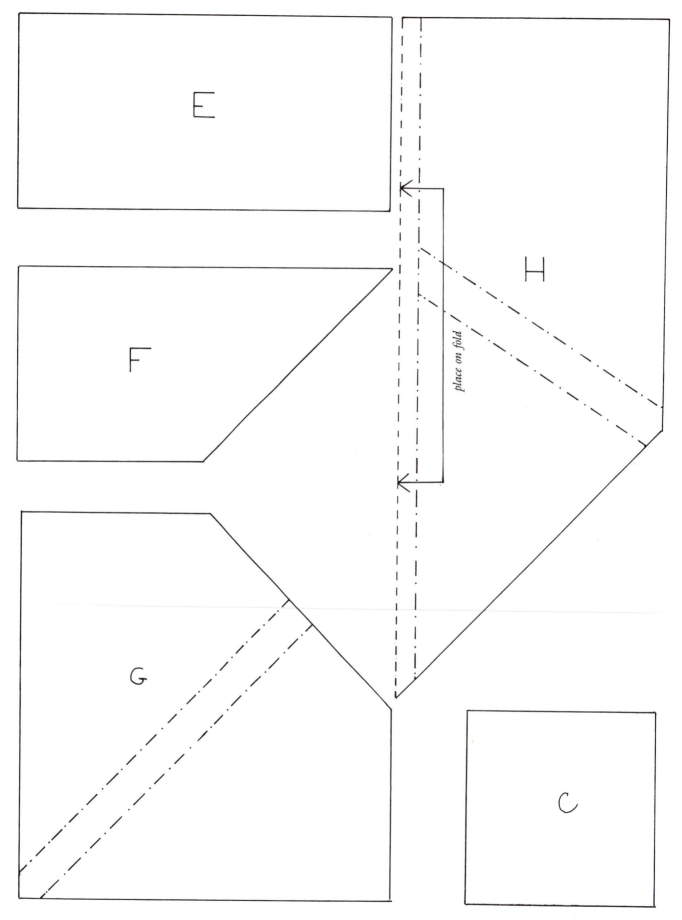

place on fold

(Fig. 148 continued.)

90

Snow Crystal

Fig. 149 Design.

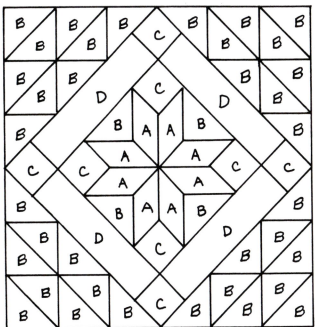

Fig. 150 Assembly diagram.

Challenging
Pieces per block: 60

A	4 light, 4 light reversed	C	4 medium, 4 dark
		D	4 light
B	12 light, 28 medium		

Use a snowy white fabric for the light pieces to create a dramatic effect. First, assemble the central square; then add the corner triangles to complete the design. Insetting is required all around the central crystal; see How to Inset.

To begin, sew each A piece to its reverse, forming

4 pairs. Sew 2 pairs together, forming each half of the crystal; press the central seams of each half in opposite directions to reduce bulk at the junction. Sew the crystal halves together, matching the seams in the middle. Inset the medium B and C pieces between the A pieces to form a square. Sew a D to opposite sides of the crystal. Sew a dark C to each end of the remaining D's; then sew to the crystal to complete the border.

Assemble the 4 corner triangles by sewing the B's together, as shown in the diagram. Sew to each edge of the crystal to complete the design.

Outline-quilt all the light pieces.

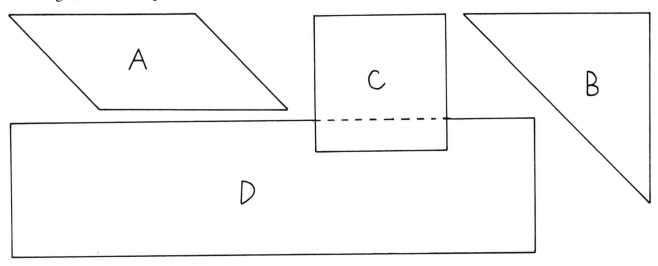

Fig. 151 Templates for Snow Crystal.

Snowflake

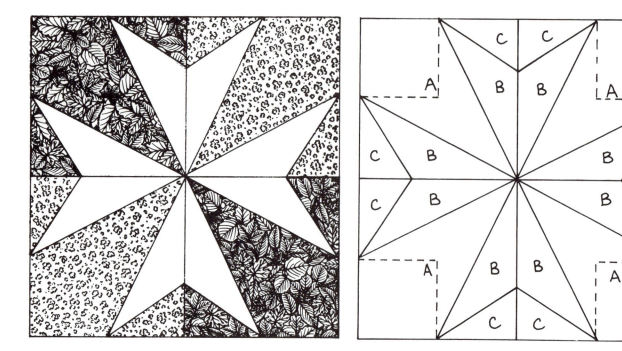

Fig. 152   Design.

Moderate
Pieces per block: 20

A   2 bright,
    2 medium

B   4 light, 4 light
    reversed

C   2 bright, 2 bright
    reversed,
    2 medium,
    2 medium reversed

A bold background vividly silhouettes the light snowflake. The design of 4 squares is simple enough. The tricky part is getting the central points to align perfectly.

Fig. 153   Assembly diagram.

Sew each B to a C. Sew B to each side of A, matching the A and C fabrics in each square. Sew 2 pairs of squares together for each half of the design; press the central seams in opposite directions to reduce bulk. Sew the halves together, matching seams carefully, to complete the design.

Outline-quilt each seam of the snowflake; quilt a square in each corner, as shown in the diagram's dotted lines.

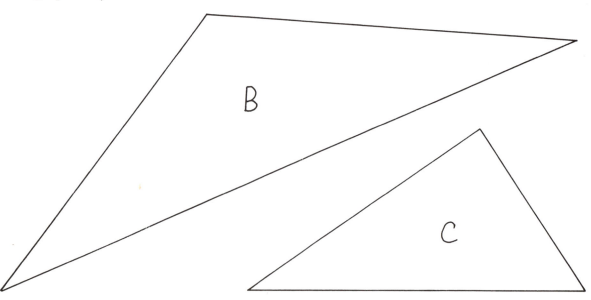

Fig. 154   Templates for Snowflake; continued on page 95.

92

Snowman

(Color page 80)

Fig. 155   Design.

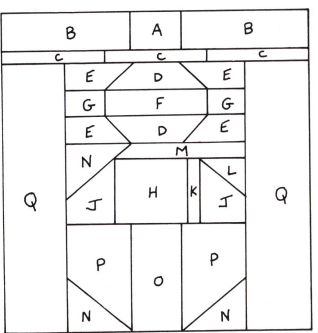

Fig. 156   Assembly diagram.

Easy
Pieces per block: 29

A	1 black	K	1 bright
B	2 sky	L	1 sky
C	1 black, 2 sky	M	1 bright
D	2 white	N	1 sky, 2 sky reversed
E	2 sky, 2 sky reversed	O	1 white
F	1 white	P	1 white, 1 white reversed
G	2 sky	Q	2 sky
H	1 white		
J	1 white, 1 white reversed		

When you embroider a carrot nose, coal-black eyes, and bright mouth and buttons, your snowman will add a cheerful note to any project. Use a blue fabric with white polka dots to simulate a snowy sky.

To make the hat, sew B to each side of A. Sew black C between the other C's, then sew to B-A-B.

For the snowman's head, sew an E to opposite sides of each D; sew G to opposite sides of F. Sew the G-F-G strip between the 2 E-D-E strips.

To make the body, sew J and K to opposite sides of H. Sew the remaining J to L; then join to K. Sew M to H-K-L; then sew N to the J-M edge. Sew P to each side of O; sew N to the angled edge of each P. Sew the 2 halves of the body together. Sew the head to the top of the body; then sew Q to each side. Sew the hat to the top of the head to complete the design.

Using 6 strands of black embroidery floss in the needle, embroider 3 French knots down the front of the body for the buttons; then with 4 strands of black, embroider knot "coals" for the eyes; then embroider a smiling mouth. Embroider a carrot nose using satin stitch and four strands of orange.

Outline-quilt the snowman, his hat and scarf; then add a row of quilting ½ inch away from the snowman.

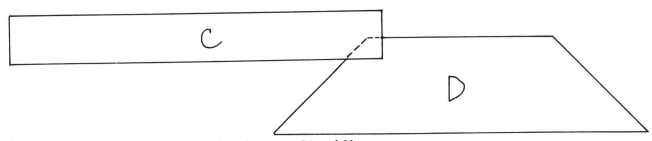

Fig. 157   Templates for Snowman; continued on pages 94 and 95.

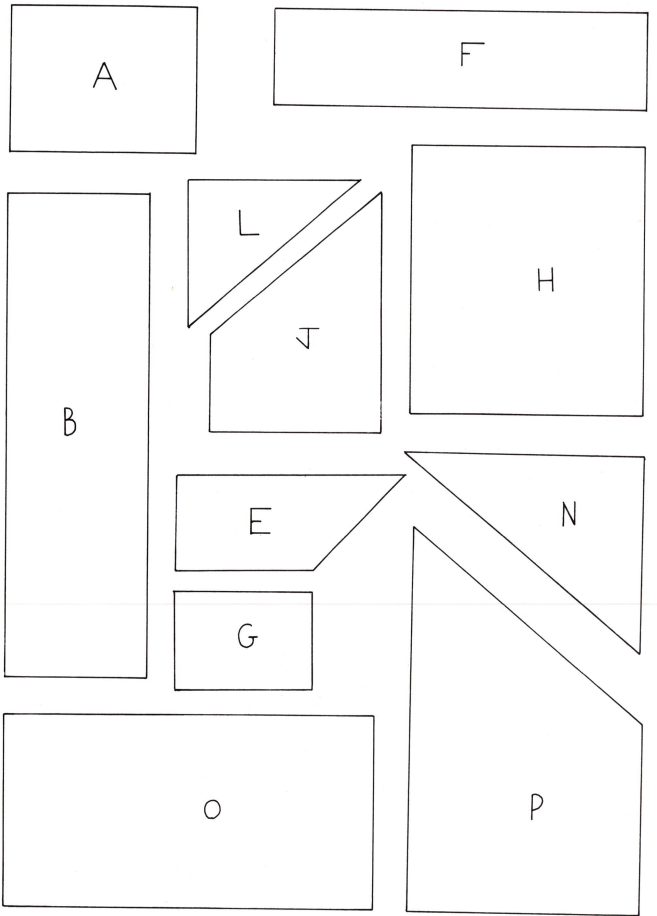

(Fig. 157 continued.)

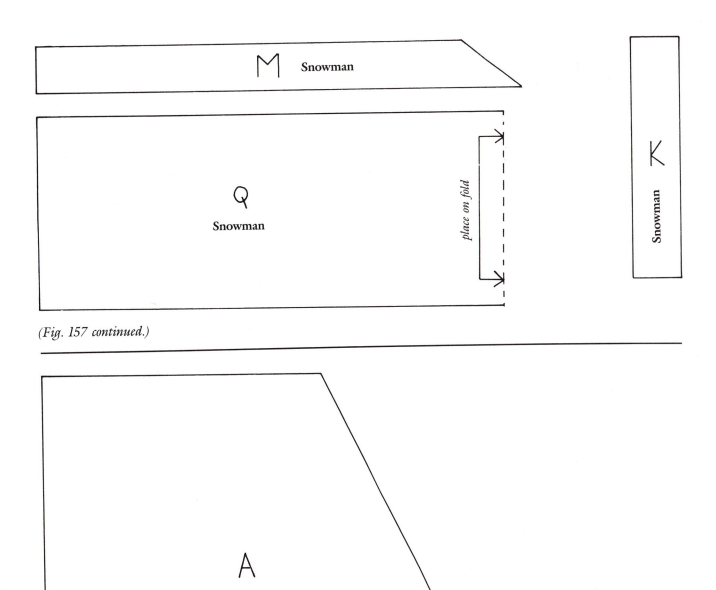

M Snowman

Q
Snowman

place on fold

Snowman K

(Fig. 157 continued.)

A

Snowflake

(Fig. 154 continued.)

Snowball Fight

(Color page 80)

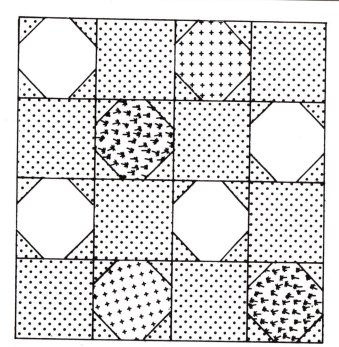

Fig. 158   Design.

Easy

Pieces per block: 48

A   8 assorted shades of
     white
B   32 blue
C   8 blue

You'll capture the excitement of a childhood snowball fight in this block. Use solid white or a selection of white prints for the A pieces. A blue polka dot fabric for the background will set off the snowballs against a snowy sky.

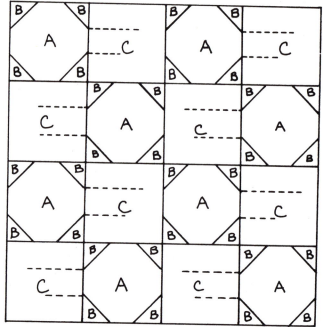

Fig. 159   Assembly diagram.

To begin, sew a B to each angled edge of each A. Arrange the A-B squares alternately with the C squares, making 4 rows with 4 squares in each row. Join the squares together in rows; then sew the rows together, matching seams carefully, to complete the design.

Quilt the outline of each snowball. Show the direction of each snowball flight by quilting straight lines to the right or left of each, as shown in the assembly diagram.

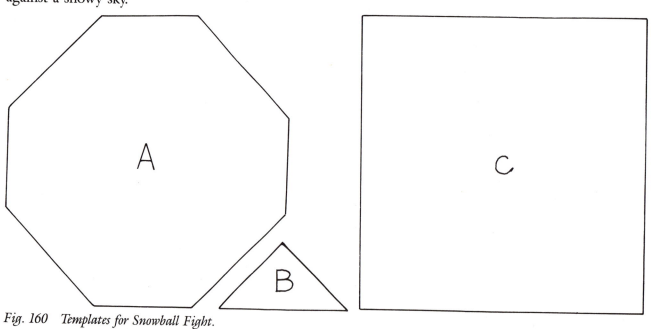

Fig. 160   Templates for Snowball Fight.

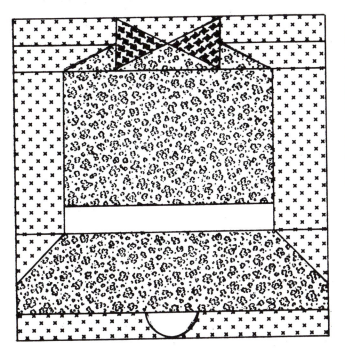

Fig. 161   Design.

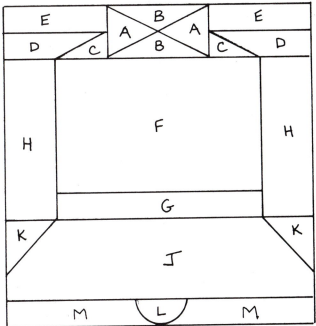

Fig. 162   Assembly diagram.

Moderate

Pieces per block: 20

A	2 dark	G	1 light
B	1 bright, 1 medium	H	2 medium
C	2 bright	J	1 bright
D	1 medium,	K	2 medium
	1 medium reversed	L	1 light
E	2 medium	M	1 medium,
F	1 bright		1 medium reversed

The only tricky part of this design is the clapper, which is sewn with a curved seam; see Sewing Curves.

To begin, sew a B to the upper right edge of one A and the lower left edge of the other A; press the seams in opposite directions to reduce bulk. Sew the A-B pairs together, matching seams carefully in the middle to complete the bow. Sew a C to the angled edge of each D. Sew D to E; then sew E-C to opposite sides of the bow.

Next, assemble the bell. Sew F to G; sew H to each side edge. Sew K to each angled edge of J; sew to H-G-H.

For the clapper, sew M to each side edge of L, keeping the strip straight. Sew to the base of the bell. Sew the bell to the bow to complete the design.

Outline-quilt the bell, bow, G strip and clapper; then add a row of quilting ½ inch away from the edges of the bell.

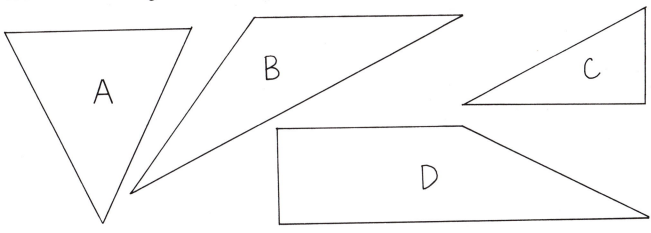

Fig. 163   Templates for Bell; continued on page 98.

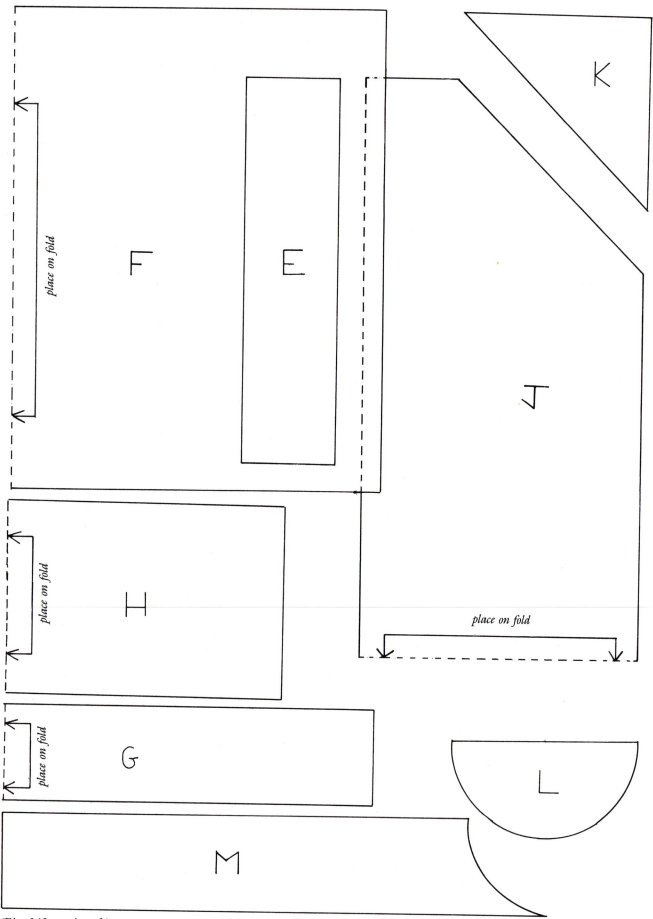

place on fold

F

E

K

J

place on fold

place on fold

H

place on fold

G

L

M

(Fig. 163 continued.)

98

Star of Bethlehem

Fig. 164   Design.

Challenging
Pieces per block: 60

A	4 medium, 4 medium reversed, 4 bright, 4 bright reversed	C	4 bright
		D	8 light
		E	4 bright, 4 bright reversed
B	20 light	F	4 dark

This variation of a traditional Christmas favorite shouldn't be tackled by beginners. Too much insetting is required for an early project using this technique; see How to Inset. As you study the design, you'll see that it is composed of 4 large squares.

To make each square: Sew a medium A to its reverse. Inset a B between the A petals; then sew a B to each side of A for the central section.

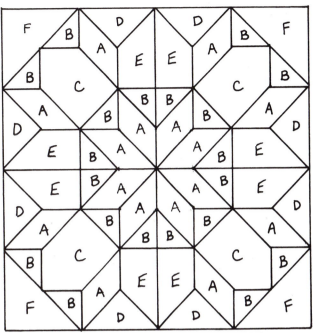

Fig. 165   Assembly diagram.

Sew a bright A to each side of C; inset a B between each of the 2 points of A-C and C-A. Sew an F to B-B. Sew an E to each bright A as shown in the diagram; inset a D between each of the two points of E-A and A-E.

Inset the central A-B section to the E-C-E edge to complete the square.

Construct the other 3 squares in the same manner. Sew 2 pairs of squares together to make each half; then sew the halves together, matching seams carefully, to complete the design.

Outline-quilt the inner and outer stars and the dark corners.

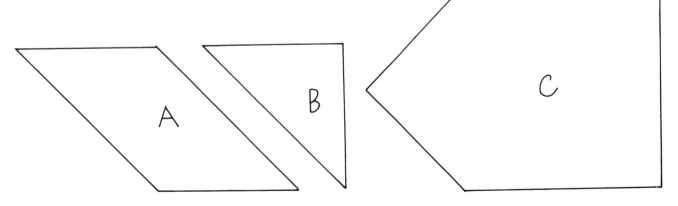

Fig. 166   Templates for Star of Bethlehem; continued on page 101.

Christmas Eve

Fig. 167   Design.

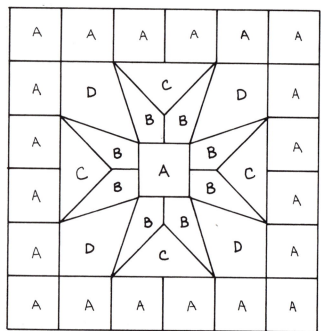

Fig. 168   Assembly diagram.

Challenging
Pieces per block: 37

A	10 bright, 11 dark	C	4 light
B	4 bright, 4 bright reversed	D	4 light

It will be quite challenging to inset the C and D pieces into the central flower. The design can be made more easily by appliquéing the central A piece in place after the adjacent B-C-D pieces have been sewn together. In any case, C must be inset into the B pieces; see How to Inset.

Sew each B piece to its reverse, forming 4 pairs of flower petals. Sew each B-B edge to the central dark A. Inset the C and D pieces between the petals to form a square. The alternative method is to sew together the B, C, and D pieces to form a ring; then appliqué the A piece over the middle.

For the border, sew the A pieces together, alternating bright and dark, and forming 2 strips of 4 squares and 2 strips of 6 squares. Sew the short strips to each side of the flower; then sew the long strips to the top and bottom to complete the design.

Outline-quilt each dark square and each of the B pieces.

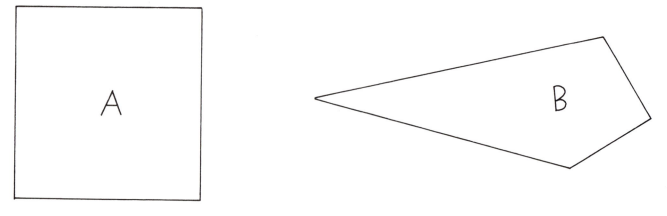

Fig. 169   Templates for Christmas Eve; continued on page 101.

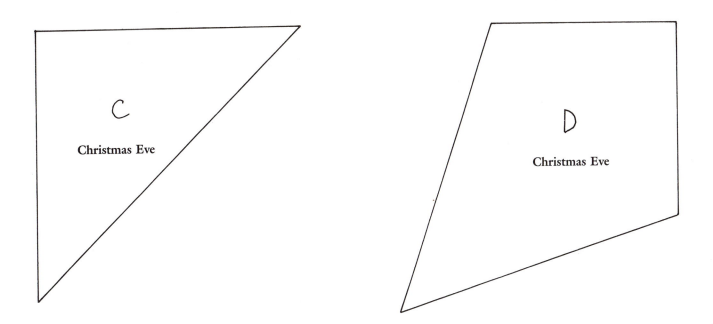

C
Christmas Eve

D
Christmas Eve

(Fig. 169 continued.)

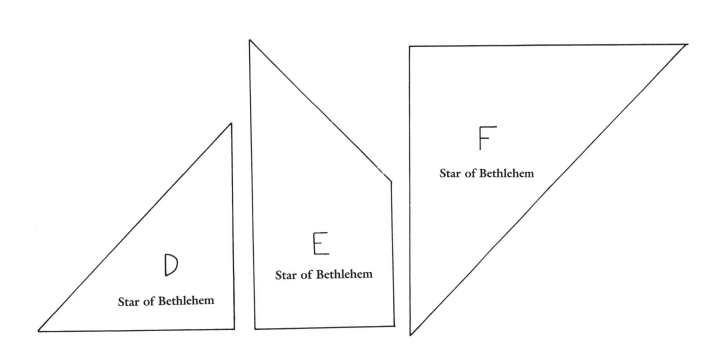

D
Star of Bethlehem

E
Star of Bethlehem

F
Star of Bethlehem

(Fig. 166 continued.)

Santa in Chimney

(Color pages 79 and 80)

Fig. 170 Design.

Easy
Pieces per block: 13

A	1 red	H	1 medium
B	1 sky	J	1 sky
C	1 sky	K	1 sky
D	1 sky	L	1 dark
E	1 white	M	1 sky
F	1 sky	N	1 white
G	1 sky		

In this design Santa is depicted squeezing down a chimney with only the top of his bright cap showing. His pompon is lightly stuffed and appliquéd to the background sky; see How to Appliqué.

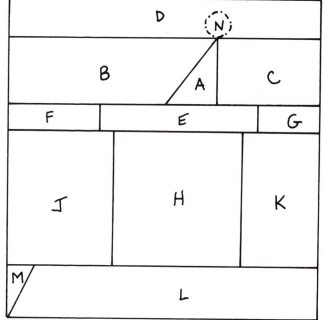

Fig. 171 Assembly diagram.

Sew B and C to opposite sides of A. Sew D to the top of the strip just made. Sew F and G to opposite sides of E; sew to B-A-C. Next, sew J and K to opposite sides of H; join to the F-E-G strip. For the roof, sew M to L; then sew to the bottom of the block to complete the patchwork part of the design.

For the pompon, hand- or machine-baste exactly on the seam line all around N. Pull the basting stitches to gather the fabric into a small cup. Place some fibrefill in the middle of the cup; then appliqué to D just above Santa's cap.

Outline-quilt around the roof, chimney, hat and pompon; then add a row of quilting ½ inch away from the first.

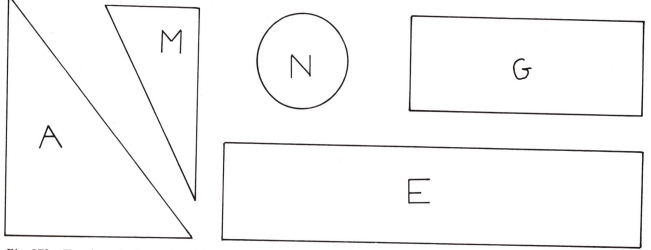

Fig. 172 Templates for Santa in Chimney; *continued on pages 103 and 106.*

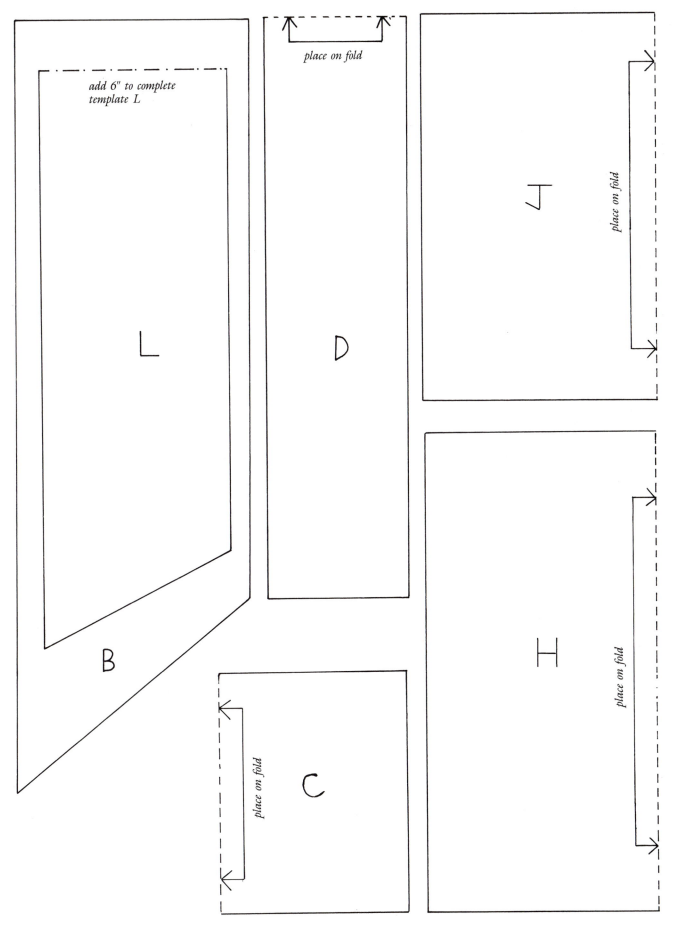

add 6" to complete
template L

place on fold

place on fold

L

D

J

B

place on fold

C

H

place on fold

place on fold

(Fig. 172 continued.)

103

Santa Claus

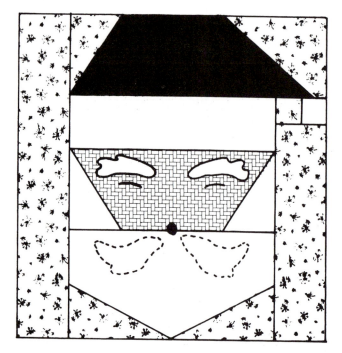

Fig. 173   Design.

Easy
Pieces per block: 14

A	1 red	F	1 white
B	1 medium	G	1 medium,
C	1 white, 1 white		1 medium reversed
	reversed, 1 medium	H	1 white, 1 medium
D	1 white, 1 medium	J	1 medium
E	1 flesh		

Santa Claus gladdens the hearts of children all over the world on Christmas Day. This patchwork image of Santa will surely add a delightful touch to a special project. Embroider the eyes and nose and appliqué the eyebrows in place; see How to Appliqué.

To begin, sew B and medium C to opposite short sides of A. Sew white D to E; then sew a white C to each angled edge of E. Sew F to C-E-C; then sew G to each angled edge of F. Sew the H pieces together; then sew to the top of medium D with the white H

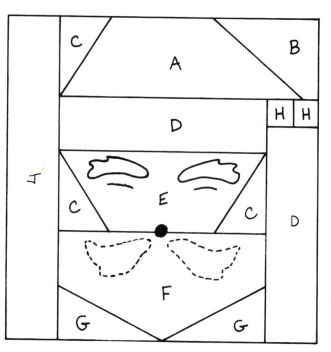

Fig. 174   Assembly diagram.

at the top right edge. Sew H-D to the right side of Santa's face; then sew the piece just made to Santa's cap. Sew J to the left edge of Santa to complete the design.

Following the instructions in How to Appliqué, prepare each of the eyebrows. Position each eyebrow on the face, as shown in the diagram; then appliqué invisibly in place, stuffing a small amount of fibrefill beneath each eyebrow for added dimension.

For the features, with 6 strands of black embroidery floss in the needle, embroider each eye using outline stitch. Using 6 strands of red floss in the needle, embroider a round nose over the face and beard with satin stitch, as shown.

Outline-quilt Santa's face, beard, cap, and pompon. Quilt his moustache on the beard, as shown in the diagram.

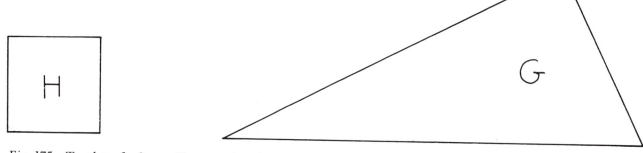

Fig. 175   Templates for Santa Claus; continued on pages 105 and 106.

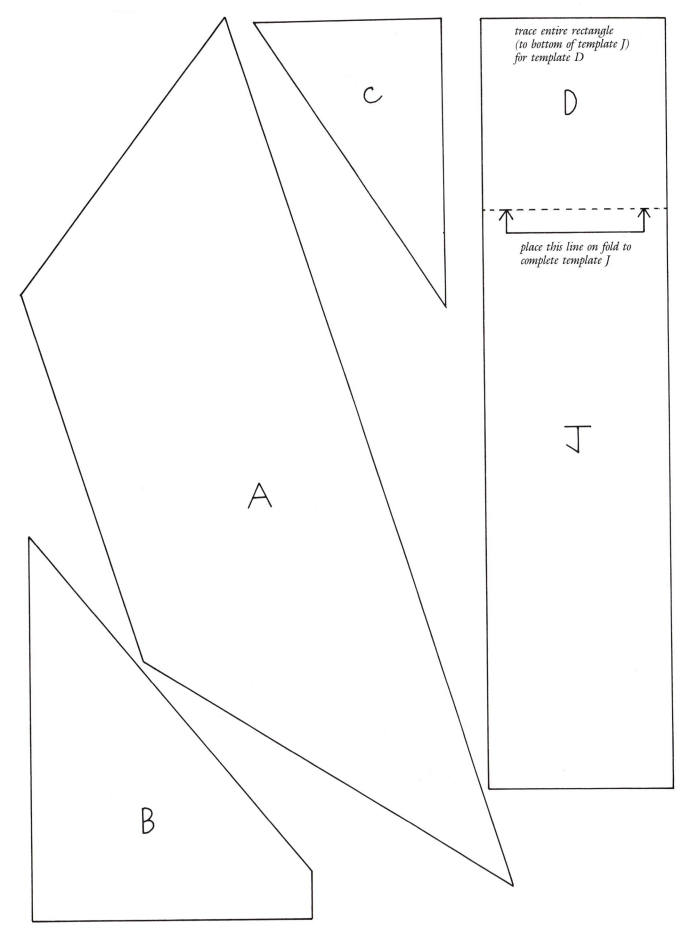

trace entire rectangle
(to bottom of template J)
for template D

D

place this line on fold to
complete template J

J

C

A

B

(Fig. 175 continued.)

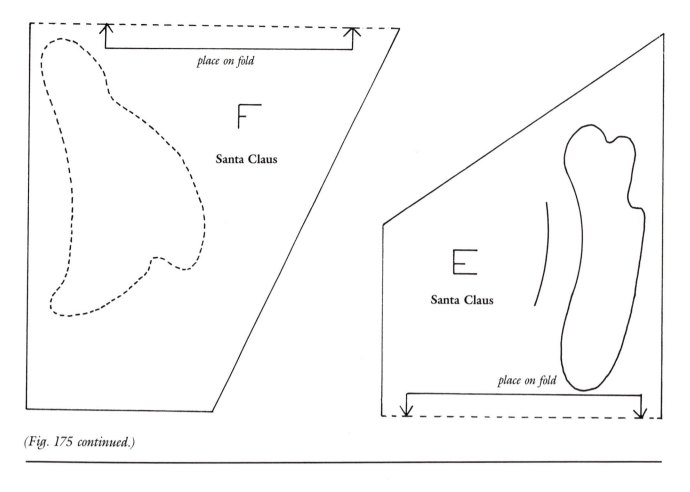

place on fold

F

Santa Claus

E

Santa Claus

place on fold

(Fig. 175 continued.)

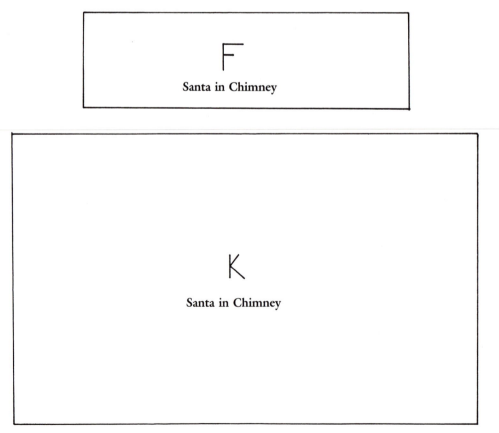

F

Santa in Chimney

K

Santa in Chimney

(Fig. 172 continued.)

December 25

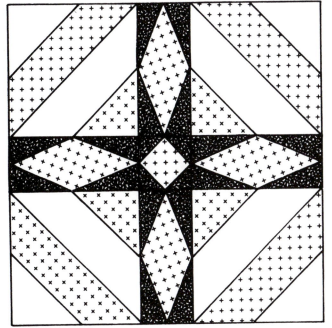

Fig. 176 Design.

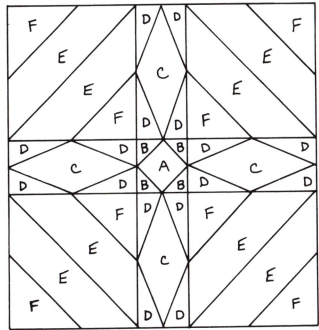

Fig. 177 Assembly diagram.

Easy
Pieces per block: 41

A	1 medium
B	4 dark
C	4 medium
D	8 dark, 8 dark reversed

E	4 light, 4 medium
F	4 light, 4 medium

Create an optical illusion—the design looks like a star at one moment or a series of diamonds the next. To achieve this effect, carefully choose the medium and dark fabrics so that they contrast well with one another. Use this design as the basis for a child's Christmas quilt. Instructions for making the quilt are on page 129.

Assemble the design in 3 horizontal strips, beginning with the central strip. Sew B to each edge of A. Sew D to each edge of 2 C's; sew the rectangles just made to each side of the central square.

Assemble the remaining C-D rectangles as described above. Sew the long edges of contrasting E's together; then sew a contrasting F to each E. Sew an E-F square to each side of each C-D rectangle for the top and bottom strips.

Sew the top and bottom strips to each side of the central strip to complete the design.

Outline-quilt the medium and dark pieces.

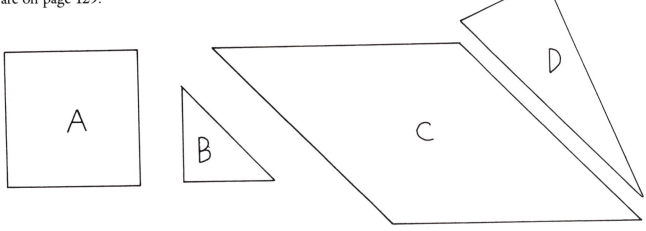

Fig. 178 Templates for December 25; continued on page 110.

Star over Bethlehem

(Color page 80)

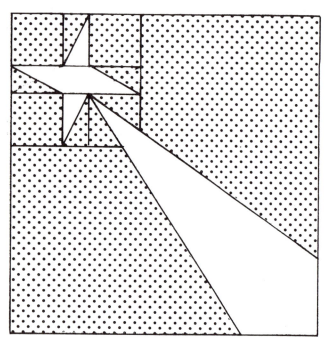

Fig. 179 Design.

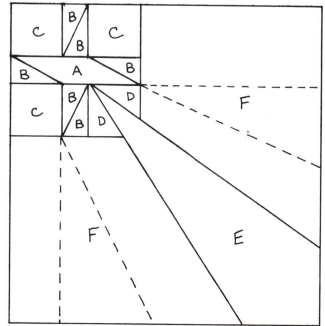

Fig. 180 Assembly diagram.

Moderate
Pieces per block: 15

A   1 light
B   2 light, 1 bright,
     3 bright reversed
C   3 bright
D   1 bright, 1 bright
     reversed

E   1 light
F   1 bright, 1 bright
     reversed

Dramatic in its simplicity, this design requires insetting of the F pieces; see How to Inset.

To begin, sew a bright B to each angled edge of

A. Sew each remaining bright B to a light B. Sew C to each side of one B-B piece for the top of the star; then sew to the A-B strip. For the bottom of the star, sew C to the left edge of the second B-B piece and D to the right edge. Sew the narrow end of E to D as shown; then sew the remaining D to E. Sew the bottom of the star to the A-B strip. Inset F into each angle formed by the star and its ray to complete the design.

Outline-quilt the star and its ray. Quilt additional lines for rays, as shown in the diagram.

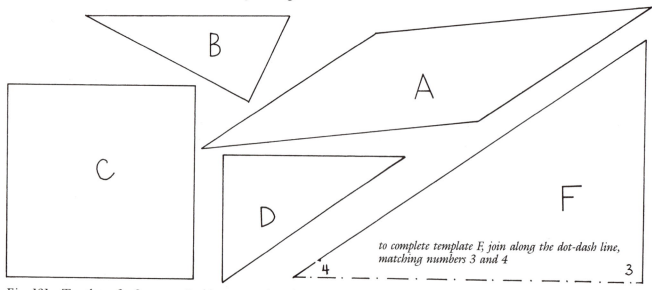

to complete template F, join along the dot-dash line, matching numbers 3 and 4

Fig. 181   Templates for Star over Bethlehem; continued on pages 110 and 111.

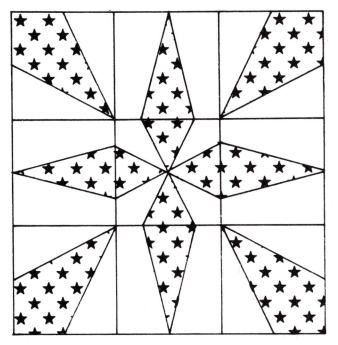

Fig. 182   Design.

Easy
Pieces per block: 32

A	4 bright	E	4 bright
B	4 medium	F	4 medium,
C	4 bright		4 medium reversed
D	4 medium,		
	4 medium reversed		

Make the star and its rays in a bright yellow fabric against a blue background for a really dramatic effect. The design is arranged in 3 rows with 3 squares in each row.

Begin with the central square. Sew each A to a B; then sew 2 pairs of A-B pieces together, forming

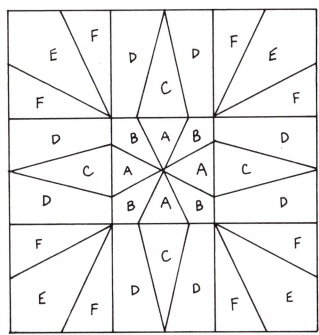

Fig. 183   Assembly diagram.

each half of the square. Press the central seams of each half in opposite directions to reduce bulk at the junction. Sew the halves of the square together, matching the seams in the middle. Next, construct the 4 side squares; sew a D to each side of each C. Finally, make the 4 corner squares by sewing an F to each side of each E.

Assemble the squares in 3 rows, as shown in the diagram. Sew the squares together in rows; then sew the rows together, matching seams carefully, to complete the design.

Outline-quilt the star and its rays; then outline-quilt again, this time ¼ inch away from each bright piece.

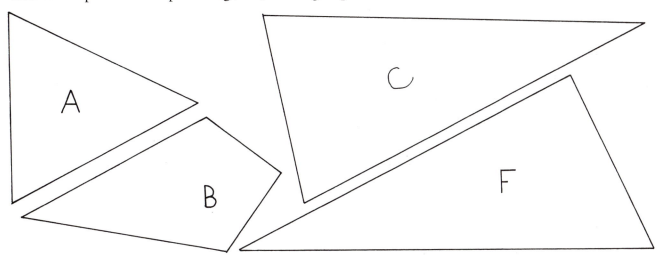

Fig. 184   Templates for Guiding Star; continued on page 111.

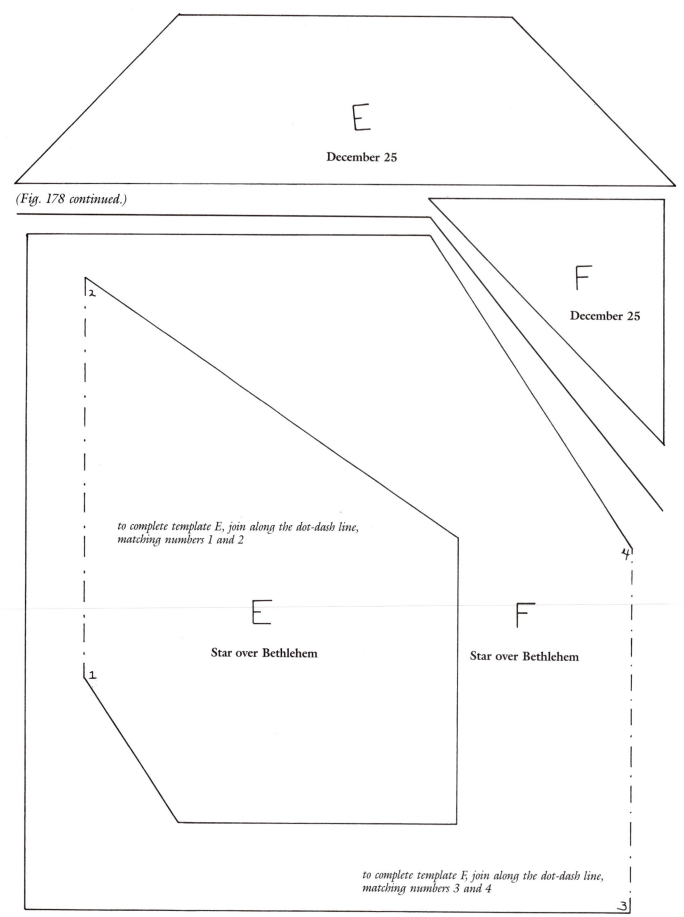

E

December 25

(Fig. 178 continued.)

2

to complete template E, join along the dot-dash line,
matching numbers 1 and 2

E

Star over Bethlehem

1

F

December 25

4

F

Star over Bethlehem

to complete template F, join along the dot-dash line,
matching numbers 3 and 4

3

(Fig. 181 continued.)

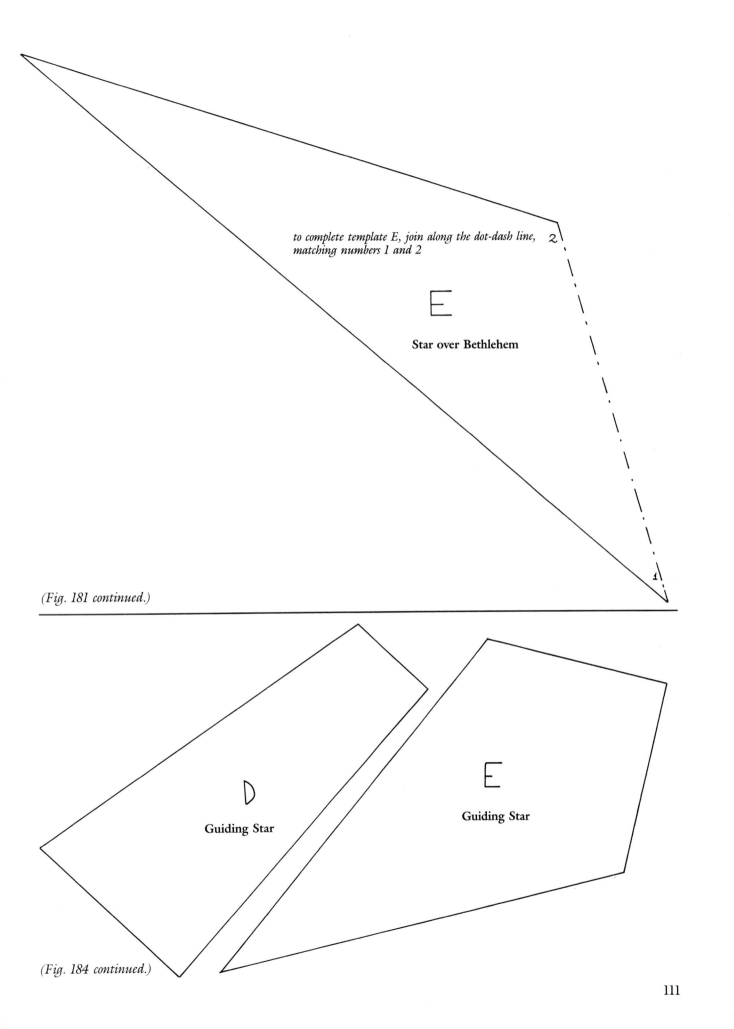

to complete template E, join along the dot-dash line,
matching numbers 1 and 2

2

E

Star over Bethlehem

1

(Fig. 181 continued.)

D

Guiding Star

E

Guiding Star

(Fig. 184 continued.)

Church

Fig. 185   Design.

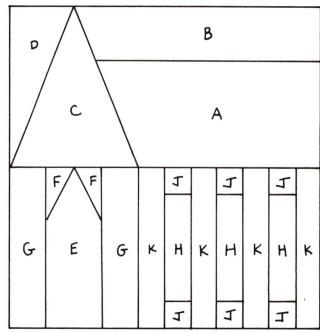

Fig. 186   Assembly diagram.

Easy
Pieces per block: 22

A	1 dark	F	1 medium,
B	1 bright		1 medium reversed
C	1 medium	G	2 medium
D	1 bright	H	3 light
E	1 light	J	6 medium
		K	4 medium

To make the upper half, sew A to B; then sew A-B to C. Sew D to the opposite edge of C. For the bottom half, sew an F to each angled edge of E. Sew a G to each side of F-E. Sew a J to each end of each H; then sew a K to each side of each J-H-J strip following the diagram. Sew K to G. Finally, sew the top to the bottom to complete the design.

Outline-quilt the roof, steeple, the door and all the windows.

Try to find a fabric that looks like wood or bricks for the church building. If you can find fabric that resembles stained glass, use it for the windows. The block is assembled in 2 halves.

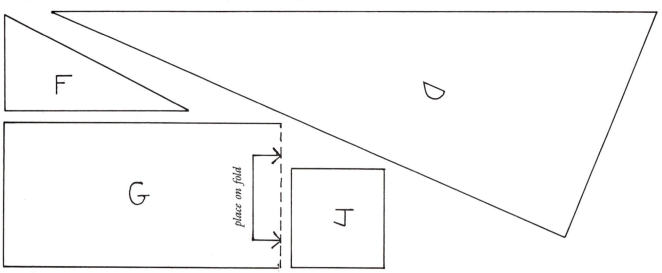

Fig. 187   Templates for Church; continued on pages 113 and 115.

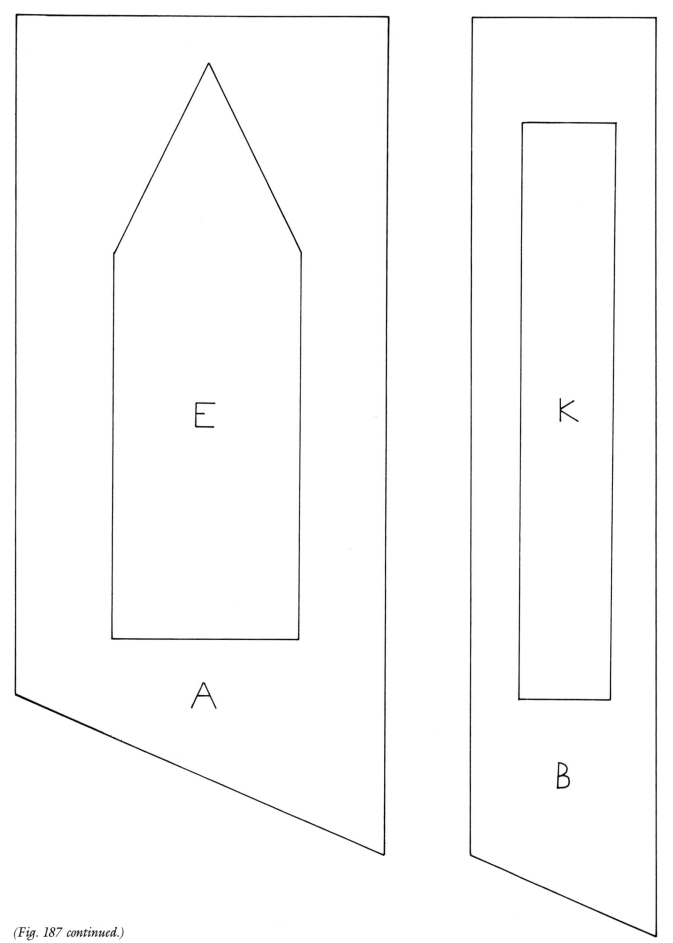

E

A

K

B

(Fig. 187 continued.)

113

Peace on Earth

(Color page 71)

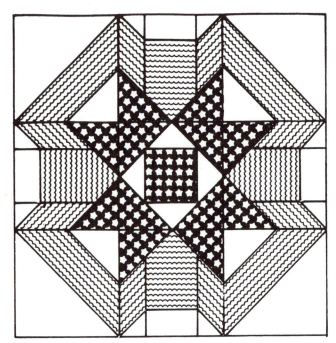

Fig. 188 Design.

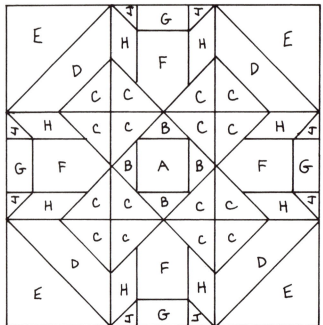

Fig. 189 Assembly diagram.

Moderate
Pieces per block: 53

A	1 dark	F	4 medium
B	4 light	G	4 light
C	4 light, 12 dark	H	4 medium,
D	4 medium		4 medium reversed
E	4 light	J	8 light

Add dimension to this design by using a pretty print with a stripe going through it for the medium pieces. Assemble the block in 3 rows with 3 squares in each row.

Begin with the central square. Sew a B to each edge of A; then sew a dark C to each B-B edge. Make the 4 corner squares next by sewing a light C to D, and D to E.

Finally, construct the 4 side squares. Sew F to G and H to J. Sew an H-J to each side of F-G. Sew a dark C to each F-H edge.

Assemble the squares in 3 rows, as shown in the diagram. Sew the squares together in rows; then sew the rows together, matching seams carefully, to complete the design.

Outline-quilt the medium and dark pieces.

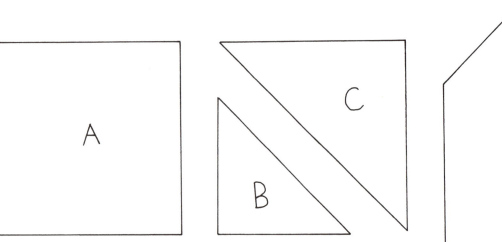

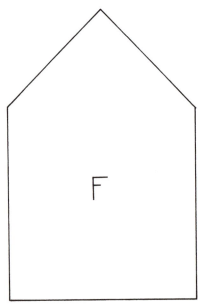

Fig. 190 Templates for Peace on Earth; continued on page 115.

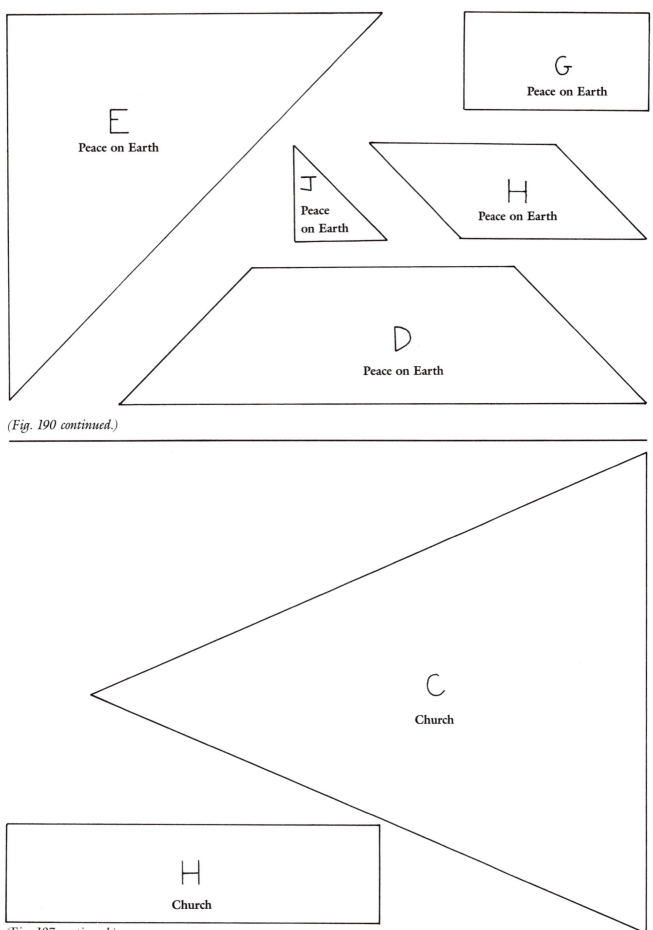

E
Peace on Earth

G
Peace on Earth

J
Peace on Earth

H
Peace on Earth

D
Peace on Earth

(Fig. 190 continued.)

C
Church

H
Church

(Fig. 187 continued.)

Projects Based on 12-Inch-Square Blocks

HOLIDAY PILLOWS

A few bright patchwork pillows piled on a bed or propped on a chair will add warmth and coziness to your holiday decorating scheme.

Select one of the following pillow designs and a design from the preceding chapter. Piece the block as directed in the individual instructions. If you wish to quilt the design before making your pillow, cut a 12½-inch-square piece of muslin (or any neutral fabric) for the back and a 12-inch-square piece of batting. See Assembling a Project for Quilting; quilt the block following the individual instructions.

Follow the requirements and individual instructions for assembling your chosen pillow style. See Ruffle, Lace, or Piping for instructions on making and attaching a ruffle, lace, or piping. After the borders, ruffles, lace or piping have been added, prepare the back in one of the suggested methods that follow.

Zipper opening: Cut the fabric to the required size; with right sides together, machine-baste the long edges together to make a ½-inch seam. (If the zipper is shorter than the length of the seam, mark off the zipper length, centered evenly between top and bottom; stitch the seam with small stitches above and below the zipper markings.) Press the seam open. Sew the zipper in place following the manufacturer's instructions (Fig. 191).

Flap opening: Cut the fabric to the required length. Press one long edge of each piece ¼ inch to the wrong side and repeat to conceal raw edges; stitch in place for a finished edge. Lap the finished edge of the smaller piece 2 inches over the larger one; baste in place at the top and bottom (Fig. 192).

When the back has been prepared, pin to the front with right sides together, raw edges even and any ruffles, lace, or piping sandwiched between them. Stitch together ¼ inch from the edges all around. Clip off each of the 4 corners at an angle, unless the pillow is round (Fig. 193); then turn to the right side. Insert the pillow form through the zipper or flap opening in the back.

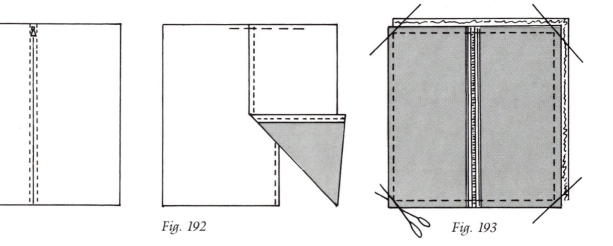

Fig. 191   Fig. 192   Fig. 193

Square Pillow with Border & Piping

(Color page 79)

Finished size: 16" square
Requirements
Block: 1   12" square
Border Fabric: 2   2½" × 12½"—¼ yard
*   2   2½" × 16½"*
Piping cord: ¼" diameter—2 yards
Piping fabric: 1   2" × 66"—⅛ yard
Back (choose one method): ½ yard
*   Zipper opening: 2   9" × 16½"*
*   Flap opening: 1   8½" × 16½"*
*   1   10½" × 16½*
Zipper (optional): 1   14" long
Pillow form: 1   16" square

Sew a short border strip to each side of the pieced block. Sew the long border strips to the top and bottom of the block. Stitch the piping to the pillow front all around.

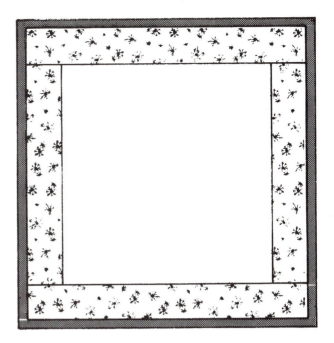

Fig. 194   Design.

Square Pillow with Border & Ruffled Trim

(Color page 79)

Finished size (excluding trim): 14" square
Requirements
Block: 12" square
Medium border fabric: 4   1½" × 12½"—⅛ yard
Bright Border fabric: 4   1½ square—scrap
Fabric for ruffle: 1   4½" × 112"—⅜ yard
Back (choose one method): ⅜ yard
*   Zipper opening: 2   8" × 14½"*
*   Flap opening: 1   7½" × 14½"*
*   1   9½" × 14½"*
Zipper (optional): 1   14" long
Pillow form: 1   14" square

Sew a bright border square to each end of 2 medium border strips. Sew a border strip to each side of the pieced block. Sew the pieced border strips to the top and bottom of the block. Stitch the ruffle to the pillow front all around. (The pillow in the color photo also has lace trim and piping; the piping was sewn first, then the lace, then the ruffle.)

Fig. 195   Design.

117

Square Pillow with Lace & Ruffled Trim (Color page 78)

Finished size (excluding trim): 12" square
Requirements
Block: 1 12" square
Lace trim: ½" wide—1½ yards
Fabric for ruffle: 4½" × 90"—¼ yard
Back (choose one method): ⅜ yard
  Zipper opening: 2 7" × 12½"
  Flap opening: 1 6½" × 12½"
      1 8½" × 12½"
Zipper (optional): 1 12" long
Pillow form: 1 12" square

First, stitch the lace to the pillow front all around; then pin the ruffle over the lace and stitch all around.

Fig. 196 Design.

Round Ruffled Pillow (Color page 78)

Finished size (excluding ruffle): 18" diameter
Requirements
Block: 1 12" square
Border fabric: ¼ yard
Fabric for ruffle: 1 6" × 175"—¾ yard
Back (choose one method): ½ yard
  Zipper opening: 2 10" × 18½"
  Flap opening: 1 9½" × 18½"
      1 11½" × 18½"
Zipper (optional): 18" long
Round pillow form: 18" diameter

Use the template to cut 4 border pieces; with right sides together, stitch the straight edges of the border pieces to the pieced block, creating a round shape. Prepare the back as directed; then center the pillow front over the back and trim away the excess fabric. Stitch the ruffle to the pillow front all around; then stitch the back in place.

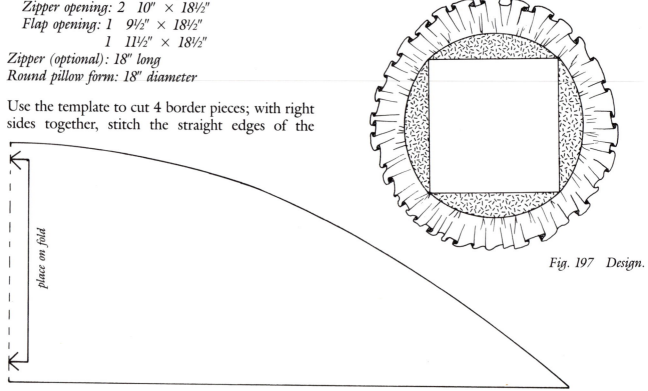

Fig. 197 Design.

place on fold

Fig. 198 Border template for Round Ruffled Pillow.

Chair Cushion

Finished size: 12" square
Requirements *for set of 6 cushions*
Blocks: 6   12" square—½ yard each of 3 to 6 fabrics
Batting*: 12   12" square
Muslin lining: 6   12½" square—¾ yard
Back: 6   12½" square—¾ yard
Binding: 24   1¼" × 12½"—⅝ yard (allows for ties)
Ties: 12   1¼" × 20"
*For a thicker cushion, use 3 layers of batting in each; you'll then require 18 squares of batting.

Comfortable chair cushions are appreciated and add charm to your dining room or kitchen. Make a set of Christmas cushions to use during the holiday season. You can repeat the same design for each cushion or vary the designs in the same color scheme.

Select one (or six!) of the 12-inch block designs from the collection in the preceding chapter. Piece the blocks, as directed in the individual instructions.

See Assembling a Project for Quilting; use the muslin lining as the back. Assemble the blocks for quilting using one piece of batting for each. Quilt each block by hand or machine, following the individual instructions.

Baste one piece of batting to the wrong side of each fabric back; if making a thicker cushion, baste 2 pieces to each back. Pin the muslin side of the quilted block to the back, sandwiching the batting between the layers; baste; then stitch together around all edges.

Prepare the binding fabric and bind all edges of

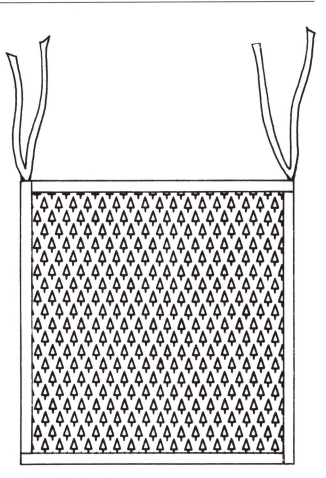

Fig. 199   Design.

each block; see Binding a Project. Make the ties; see Loops & Ties. Slip-stitch the middle of each tie to the 2 top corners of each cushion.

Decorations

You'll find many block designs in the preceding chapter from which you can create attractive, unusual decorations. Brighten your doors, windows, and walls with them. You can adapt the block designs into delightful, three-dimensional shapes. Some designs—Cat, Santa Claus, Snowman, for example—can be transformed into toys. Many elements that had made a design challenging in the design chapter have been omitted. Background templates surrounding each motif have been eliminated to simplify the construction. Whipping them up will be fun and even a beginner can tackle most of these projects.

The small assembly diagrams provided with each design show the shape and position of the required templates. Refer to the screened diagrams of the block design in the preceding chapter to select the appropriate fabrics for each template. Each design below lists the templates needed to complete it. The number (in parentheses) following each letter refers to the number of pieces required; only one piece is required for letters without a number.

Cut out the fabric pieces using the templates, the list, and screened diagram for the appropriate colors. Arrange the pieces on a flat surface, following the assembly diagram. Stitch together, as directed in the individual instructions; ignore the instructions for the pieces that have been omitted. Use the pieced front as a pattern to cut out a piece in reverse for the back; cut it from a scrap of matching fabric.

For a special detail, trim the edges of the pieced front with lace or piping using instructions under Lace or Piping.

With right sides together and raw edges even, stitch the front to the back with the optional lace or piping sandwiched between them; leave a 3-inch opening to turn right side out. (For the Holly Wreath, you won't need an opening; just stitch together completely around the outside edges. See Patchwork Wreaths for instructions on stuffing and finishing.) Clip into the seam allowance at any curves or angled edges; trim off any points or corners. Turn the project to the right side and stuff with fibrefill until plump. If you are making a toy, stuff until it is quite firm. Fold the raw edges at the opening ¼-inch inside and slip-stitch the opening to close.

Add dimension to your door or window decoration by sewing through the front, batting and back at strategic points, making a tufting stitch; see Tufting Stitch. Sew a hook or loop to the back of the decoration.

Design templates and number of pieces
Home for the Holidays: 16   A, B, D, F, G, H(4), J(2), K, L(2), M(2)
Holly Wreath: 24   A(8), D(8), E(8)
Christmas Star: 52   A(4), B(32), C(16)
Cat: 11   B(2), G, L(2), M, N, O, U, W(2)
Yuletide Cheer: 28   A(4), B(4), C(4), D(4), E(8), F(4)
Christmas Tree: 6   A, C, E, G, J, L
Stocking: 9   A, B, C, D, F, G, H(3)
Gift: 13   A(2), B, C(2), D, F(4), G(2), H
Candle: 11   A, C, E, G(3), H(2), K(2), M
Snow Crystals: 24   A(8), B(4), C(8), D(4)
Snowman: 13   A, C, D(2), F, H, J(2), K, M, O, P(2)
Bell: 9   A(2), B, C(2), F, G, J, L
Santa Claus: 9   A, C(2), D, E, F, H, J(2)
Star of Bethlehem: 40   A(16), B(12), C(4), E(8)
Peace on Earth: 37   A, B(4), C(16), D(4), F(4), H(8)

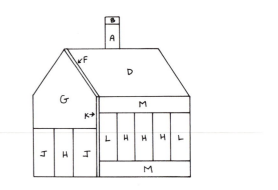

Home for the Holidays

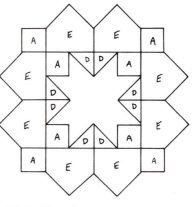

Holly Wreath

Fig. 200 Assembly diagrams; continued on page 121.

120

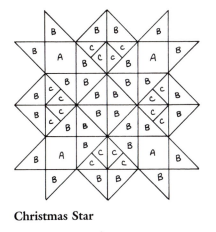

Christmas Star

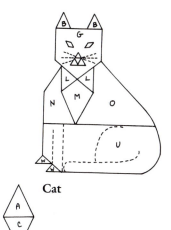

Cat

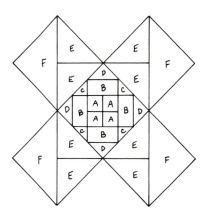

Yuletide Cheer

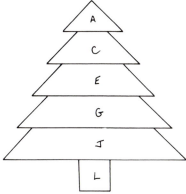

Christmas Tree

Candle

Stocking

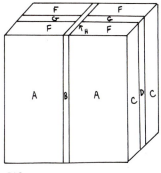

Gift

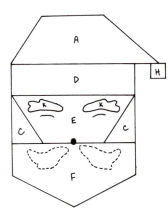

Santa Claus

Snow Crystal

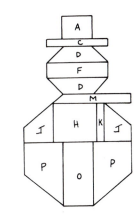

Snowman

Star of Bethlehem

Bell

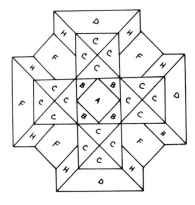

Peace on Earth

(Fig. 200 continued.)

Writing Caddy

Finished size: 12" square
Requirements
Block: 1   12" square—scraps, 3 to 6 fabrics
Muslin lining: 1   12½" square—scrap or ⅜ yard
Batting: 2   12" square
Back (fabric A): 1   12½" square—⅜ yard*
Ruffled lace trim: ½" wide—2¼ yards
Ties (fabric A): 2   1" × 12"
Sturdy cardboard: 2   12" square
Interior (fabric B): 2   12½" square—⅜ yard*
Pockets: 2   6" × 9"
Fabric A: 6   3½" square
Fabric C: 6   3½" square—¼ yard*
Lining (fabric C): 2   6½" × 9½"
Penholder (fabric A): 1   1½" × 4½"
Stamp holder (fabric C)
Pocket: 1   3½" square
Flap: 1   2½" × 3½"
Button: 1   ⅜"
*Total amount needed for entire project.

Fig. 201   Writing Caddy (closed).

Since moving to England, I rely on letters rather than telephone calls to family and friends. Now I realize the value of having a small book or caddy for my vital writing supplies: envelopes, stationery, pen, stamps, and letters to be answered. Not finding a suitable one in any shop, I designed this one myself!

Make the caddy as an unusual Christmas gift for an avid letter-writing friend (or as a gentle hint to someone who doesn't write often enough). Of course, you can always make it for yourself, but then you'll no longer have an excuse for not writing letters!

Select a design from the preceding chapter. Piece the block as directed in the individual instructions. See directions under Assembling a Project for Quilting; use the muslin lining piece as the back. Quilt the block by hand or machine, following the individual instructions.

To assemble the exterior of the caddy, baste the second piece of batting to the back (fabric A). With right sides together and raw edges even, stitch the quilted front to the padded back, making a ¼-inch seam. (If your quilted design faces in a definite direction, such as the bell or candle, be sure to stitch the seam along the left edge so that the design is correctly positioned when the caddy is finished.)

Next, sew the ruffled lace trim to the exterior. With raw edges even, pin the lace to the edge of the exterior all around, making a large pleat at each corner. Stitch the lace to the exterior, making a ¼-inch seam. Slip-stitch the ends together.

Next, make 2 ties; see Loops & Ties for directions. Baste one end of each tie to the midpoint of the front and back sides, as shown in the diagram. Now assemble the interior. First, with right sides together and raw edges even, sew the two 12½-inch squares together.

To make the pockets, arrange the 3½-inch squares, alternating colors, checkerboard style, as shown in the assembly diagram, to form 2 groups with 6 in in each. Sew the squares together in rows with 3 squares in each row. Sew 2 pairs of rows together, matching seams carefully, to make each pocket. With right sides together and raw edges even, stitch each of the pockets to a lining as follows: For the envelope pocket, stitch together along the top and right side; for the stationery pocket, stitch along the top and sides. Turn to the right side and press. Pin and baste to the interior with raw edges even, as shown in the diagram. Topstitch the pockets in place along the sides; then stitch a line down the middle of the envelope pocket, as shown with a dotted line.

For the penholder, hem one short edge; then press the 2 long edges ¼ inch to the wrong side. Pin and baste to the interior with raw edges even, following the assembly diagram. Topstitch each long edge in place.

For the stamp pocket, hem one edge for the top of the pocket; then press the left and bottom edge ¼ inch to the wrong side. Pin and baste to the interior with raw edges even as shown in the diagram. Top-stitch the left and bottom edges in place. To make the flap, fold the fabric in half lengthwise with right sides facing and raw edges even. Stitch across the long edge and one short edge. Turn to the right side, fold the raw end inside and slip-stitch in place; press. Make a ½-inch buttonhole in the middle of the flap. (A snap or small piece of Velcro fastening tape can be used instead of a button.) Pin the flap to the interior so that it overlaps the stamp pocket;

slip-stitch the top edge in place. Sew the button to the pocket.

With right sides together and raw edges even, pin the interior and exterior together, sandwiching the lace and ties between them and leaving the back edge open. Stitch together ¼ inch form the edges. Turn to the right side. To give the caddy support and enable you to fold it in half, tape the 2 pieces of cardboard together to make a "hinge." Insert the folded cardboard inside the caddy. Turn the raw edges along the back edge inside and slip-stitch securely together, enclosing the cardboard.

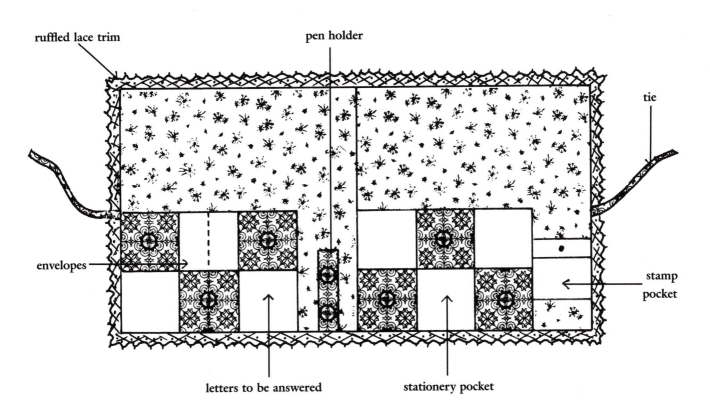

Fig. 202   Writing Caddy (open).

TABLE RUNNER

Place this runner on your dining room or kitchen table between meals during the holiday season for a very special feeling of Christmas cheer.

The requirements and instructions below are for the 3-Block Runner. Adapt the design to fit your own table size; see the chart below to determine the number of blocks and side triangles you'll need. Adjust the amount of fabric and batting that you purchase in accordance with the size of the runner you plan to make.

Table Runner Chart		
blocks	side triangles	total length
2	2	34"
3	4	51"
4	6	68"
5	8	85"

3-Block Runner

(Color pages 68 and 69)

Finished size: 17" × 51"
Requirements
Blocks: 3   12" square—¼ yard each of 4 or 5 fabrics
Background: 1½ yards (includes fabric for the back)
   Sides (right-angle triangles): 4   12½" × 12½" × 17½"
   End strips (optional): 4   1" × 12½"
Back: 1   19" × 53"—(see Background)
Batting: 1   17" × 51"
Separate binding (optional): 1   1" × 116"—¼ yard

Select 3 compatible designs from the preceding chapter's collection; sew the patchwork, as directed in the individual instructions.

After the blocks have been completed, sew a side triangle to the upper left and lower right edge of block 2 with right sides together and raw edges even. Then sew a side triangle to the lower right edge of block 1 and the upper left edge of block 3 in the same manner. Matching seams carefully, sew the 3 strips just made together. If you like, sew the end strips to the raw edges of blocks 1 and 3. The end strips should only be added if you are fold-finishing the table runner.

Finishing: See Assembling a Project for Quilting; quilt each of the blocks, following the individual instructions. Select one of the background quilting designs given here; then quilt each of the side triangles. Bind the runner, following your chosen method; see Binding a Project. Fabric has been allowed for self-binding the project; if you are adding a separate binding, trim the back so it is even with the top of the runner; the proceed.

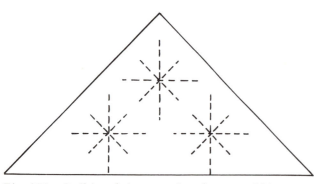
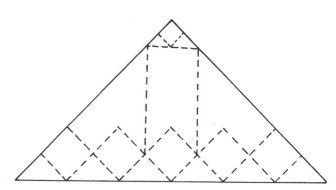

Fig. 203   Quilting designs; continued on page 204.

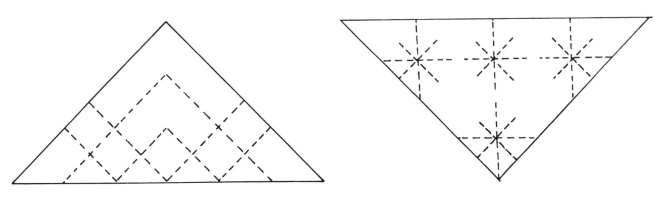

(Fig. 203 continued.)

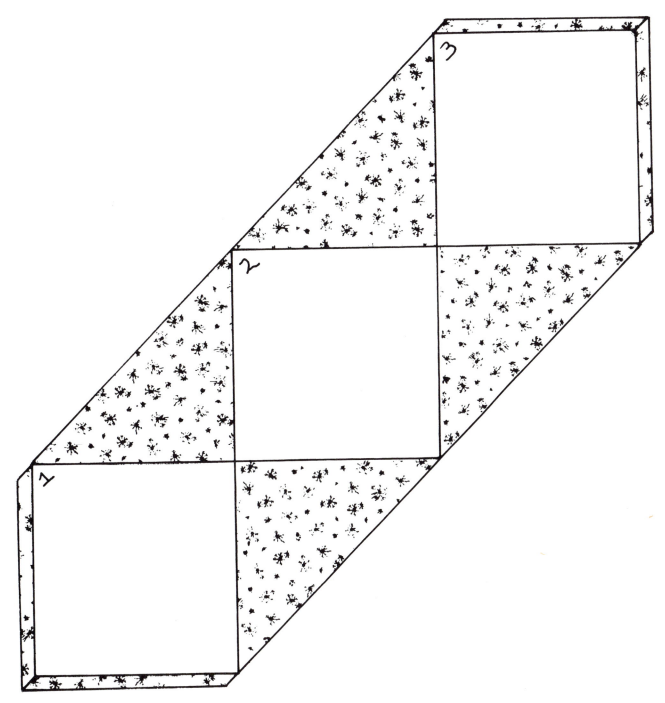

Fig. 204   Table Runner design.

Sampler Quilt

Whether you hang this quilt on a wall or spread it on your bed, it will radiate the warmth and happiness of the holidays to all who see it.

Select patchwork designs that have a special meaning for you from the collection in the preceding chapter. Do you share your home with a cat or dog? Then make the appropriate block (Cat or Dog) and position it in a place of honor on your quilt. Do you live in a region where Christmas Day is warm and sunny? How about a variety of snow-related designs—Snowman, Snowball Fight, Snow Crystal, Snowflake—for a white Christmas! Add an assortment of bells, candles, wreaths, trees and stars. Your quilt will be a joyous celebration of the holiday season.

Choose either of these quilt sizes; each size has its own requirements, indicating how much fabric and batting you'll need. For the blocks, I listed the yardage needed for 6 different fabrics to create a quiet, elegant quilt. For a fun quilt, fill in with fabric scraps to add special highlights and splashes of color. The quilt in the color photo was pieced from my abundant scrap basket with only a few new purchases. Search through your own scraps for vibrant fabrics that shout "Christmas"; then fill in with some new prints bought specially for your Christmas quilt.

Another way to add spice to your quilt: Frame the blocks with contrasting fabrics, checkerboard style, as shown in the assembly diagram for the 16-Block Quilt. By experimenting with colors you may find that some blocks are enhanced by a light fabric frame, while others by a dark fabric. The requirements provide the option of framing all the blocks in one fabric or in two different ones.

Just another reminder before you begin following the instructions below: Sign and date your quilt either on the back or the front. An excellent way to sign your name on the front is to incorporate your signature into the block design; see Stocking and Message Block.

To make your quilt, select one of the quilt designs that follow; then choose the appropriate number of 12-inch blocks from the preceding chapter. Piece each block, as directed in the individual instructions.

After completing the blocks, clear a large flat surface and arrange the blocks in rows, following the assembly diagram for the quilt you are making. Study your arrangement to see how the designs look next to one another. The range of colors and prints should be evenly balanced throughout the quilt; check for areas where you have a preponderance of one color or print and move the block to a more pleasing position. The corners and middle are key spots in your quilt; try to position your most attractive or most meaningful blocks in these places. Keep moving the blocks around, and critically study the effects until you are completely satisfied with your arrangement. Be sure to make a note of your final decision on the assembly diagram, or pin the blocks together in rows unless you have an excellent memory! If you are framing the blocks with different fabrics, decide upon the frame color for each.

To assemble the quilt top, sew the short frames in place first; then sew the longer frames to the block and short frames. Join the blocks in rows with the vertical sashing, as shown in the assembly diagram.

For the horizontal sashing, using a pencil and ruler, mark off the position of the seams to which the sash will be attached. (This is where sashing will help you to maintain accuracy in your quilt top.) Then sew the framed blocks and vertical sashing to the long sash, matching your markings to the seams. For example, if you are making the 16-block quilt, mark off ¼ inch for the outer seam allowance; measure 14 inches and mark off the edge of the first block. Mark off 2 inches for the vertical sash; then mark off another 14 inches for the second block. Continue across the sash until you have marked the final ¼ inch for the remaining seam allowance.

When sewing the sashing in place, match up your markings accurately to the seams. Don't be tempted to trim off excess from the end of the sash to make it come out even! Press carefully when finished.

Finishing: See Assembling a Project for Quilting for necessary instructions. Quilt each of the blocks following the individual instructions. Outline-quilt each of the frames. Select quilting patterns for the corners, intersections, sashing, and border of your quilt. Bind the quilt following your chosen method; see Binding a Project. Fabric has been allowed for self-binding the quilt. If you are adding a separate binding, trim the back so it is even with the quilt top; then proceed.

16-Block Quilt

(Color page 80)

Finished size: 70" square
Requirements
Blocks: 16   12" square—1 yard each of 6 fabrics
Frames: 1" wide—1¼ yards or ¾ yard each of 2
fabrics
   Horizontal: 32   1½" × 14½"
   Vertical: 32   1½" × 12½"
Sashing: 2" wide—1¾ yards*
   Horizontal: 3   2½" × 62½"
   Vertical: 12   2½" × 14½"
Border: 4   4½" × 70½"—2 yards
Back (allows for self-binding): 2   37" × 72½"—4
yards
Batting: 70" square
Separate binding (optional): 1   2" × 284"—½ yard
*Buy only 2 yards if you are making the sashing and the
border from the same fabric.

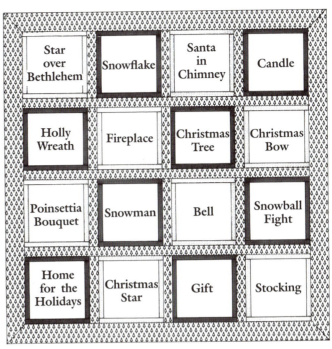

Fig. 205   16-Block Quilt design.

20-Block Quilt

Finished size: 76" × 92"
Requirements
Blocks: 20   12" square—1½ yards each of 6 fabrics
Frames: 1" wide—1¼ yards or ¾ yard each of 2
fabrics
   Horizontal: 40   1½" × 12½"
   Vertical: 40   1½" × 14½"
Sashing: 2" wide—2 yards*
   Horizontal: 6   2½" × 66½"
   Vertical: 25   2½" × 14½"
Border: pieced
   Inner horizontal: 2   1½" × 68½" ⎫
   Inner vertical: 2   1½" × 84½"   ⎬—2⅜ yards*
   Outer horizontal: 2   4½" × 76½" ⎫
   Outer vertical: 2   4½" × 92½"   ⎬—2⅝ yards
Back (allows for self-binding): 2   41" × 94½"—5¼
yards
Batting: 1   76" × 92"
Separate Binding (optional): 1   2" × 344"—½ yard
*Buy only 2⅝ yards if you are making the sashing and
the outer border from the same fabric. You can avoid
buying extra fabric by making the inner border and the
back from the same fabric; if you decide to do this, buy
only 5¼ yards.

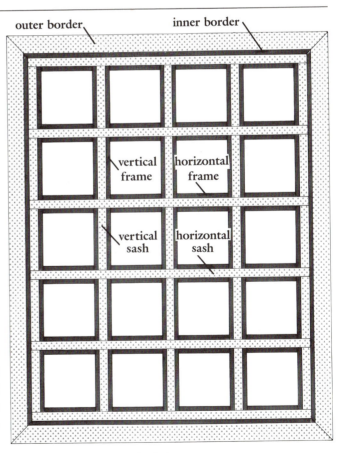

Fig. 206   20-Block Quilt design.

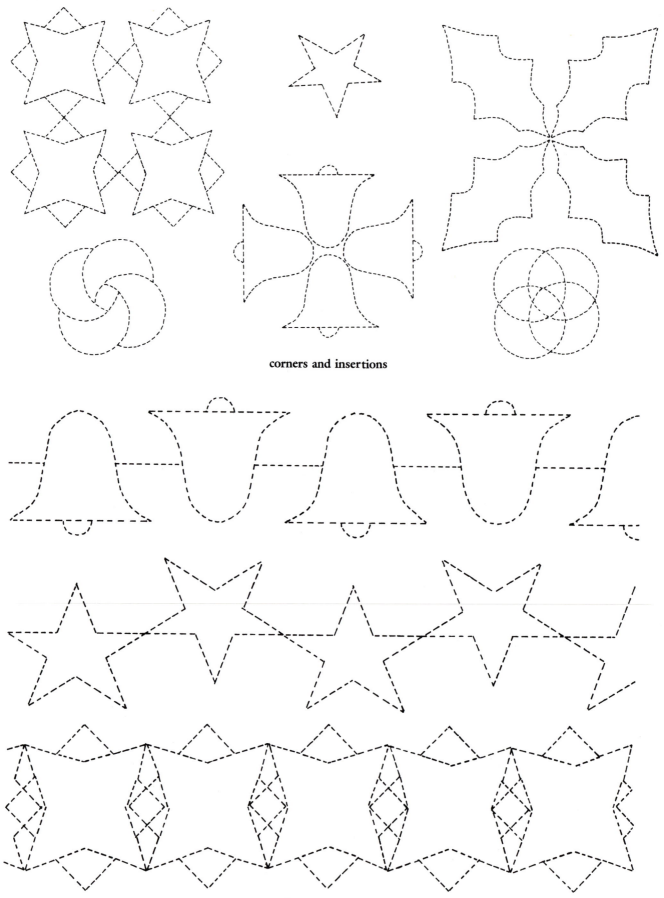

corners and insertions

sashes and borders

Fig. 207   Quilting designs; continued on page 129.

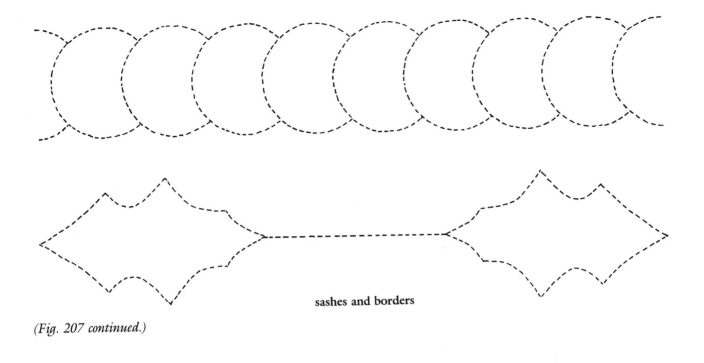

sashes and borders

(Fig. 207 continued.)

Child's Quilt

Easy
Finished size: 26" × 33"
Requirements
Fabric
   Light: ½ yard
   Medium: ⅜ yard
   Dark: ⅜ yard*
Back (allows for self-binding): 1   28½ × 35½"—1 yard*
Batting: 1   26" × 33"
Separate binding (optional): 1   1" × 122"—¼ yard
*Only 1 yard of the dark fabric is required if you are making the back and the pieced stars from the same fabric.
Pieces per quilt: 295

A	12 light	E	20 light, 20 medium
B	48 dark		
C	31 light	F	20 light, 20 medium
D	62 dark, 62 dark reversed		

Give your favorite child a special quilt to snuggle beneath on the night before Christmas (and all through the rest of the year)! This simple design is very easy to piece. Use the templates for the December 25 block in the preceding chapter.

Assemble the quilt first in units, then in rows. First, construct each of the units: Sew a B to each edge of A, forming a square. Sew a D to each edge of C, forming a rectangle. Sew the long edges of contrasting E's together; then sew a contrasting F to each E, forming a square.

Arrange these units in rows, following the assembly diagram; note that the only difference between rows 1 and 3 is the angle of the E-F squares.

Row 1 (make 3): Sew an E-F square to each side of 2 C-D rectangles. Join the 2 strips just made to a central C-D rectangle to complete the row.

Row 2 (make 4): Sew a C-D rectangle to each side of 2 A-B squares. Join the 2 strips just made to a central A-B square to complete the row.

Row 3 (make 2): Construct as for Row 1, angling the E-F squares in the opposite direction.

Sew the rows together following the assembly diagram and matching seams carefully to complete the quilt top.

Finishing: See Assembling a Project for Quilting for necessary instructions. Quilt each of the E-F units following the assembly diagram; outline-quilt each of the stars. Bind the quilt following your chosen method; see Binding a Project. Fabric has been allowed for self-binding the quilt; if you are adding a separate binding, trim the back so that it is even with the quilt top; then proceed.

Fig. 208   Child's Quilt design.

Fig. 209   Child's Quilt assembly diagram.

"I'll Be Home for Christmas" Wall Hanging *(Color pages 72 and 73)*

This wall hanging will stimulate your creativity. It can be as simple or elaborate, large or small, easy or challenging as you make it. You are the designer!

It is up to you to select major components, as shown on the design diagram; you have a choice

between 2 stars for the upper border, and a wreath or evergreen for the lower border. There are 6 different small stars you can feature in the sky; these vary from simple to challenging. If one of the star designs is too difficult, simply replace it with an easy

Fig. 210 Design.

132

one. You can repeat the same star 6 times, repeat 3 stars twice, feature the complete illustrated selection, or decided on another variation.

For the large star, there are 6 different designs from which to choose; these range from easy to challenging and it's up to you to pick the star you'd like to feature. Below the mountains on the left, you can include the Christmas tree as I have, or create a forest of small evergreens.

The unchangeable parts of the design are the mountains, forest section, house, and fence. You can make a smaller wall hanging, however, by eliminating the border; if you decide to do this, you can also omit the mountains or fence strip, if you wish. Have

Fig. 211 Assembly diagram.

fun and use your imagination with this project. You will be rewarded with a work of art to treasure for many Christmases to come.

Finished size (as shown): 34" × 39"

Requirements

Sky (blue fabric with white polka dots): ½ yard
  Background squares: 6 4½" × 4½"

Upper border: 1 3½" × 4½"
Upper border: 8 3½" × 3½"
Mountains (blue or purple): ¼ yard
Field (green print on white): ⅛ yard
Stars (yellow, gold, white): ¼ yard of 2 yellows; scraps of 3 other colors
Trees (green): ¼ yard of 2 greens; scraps of 2 other prints

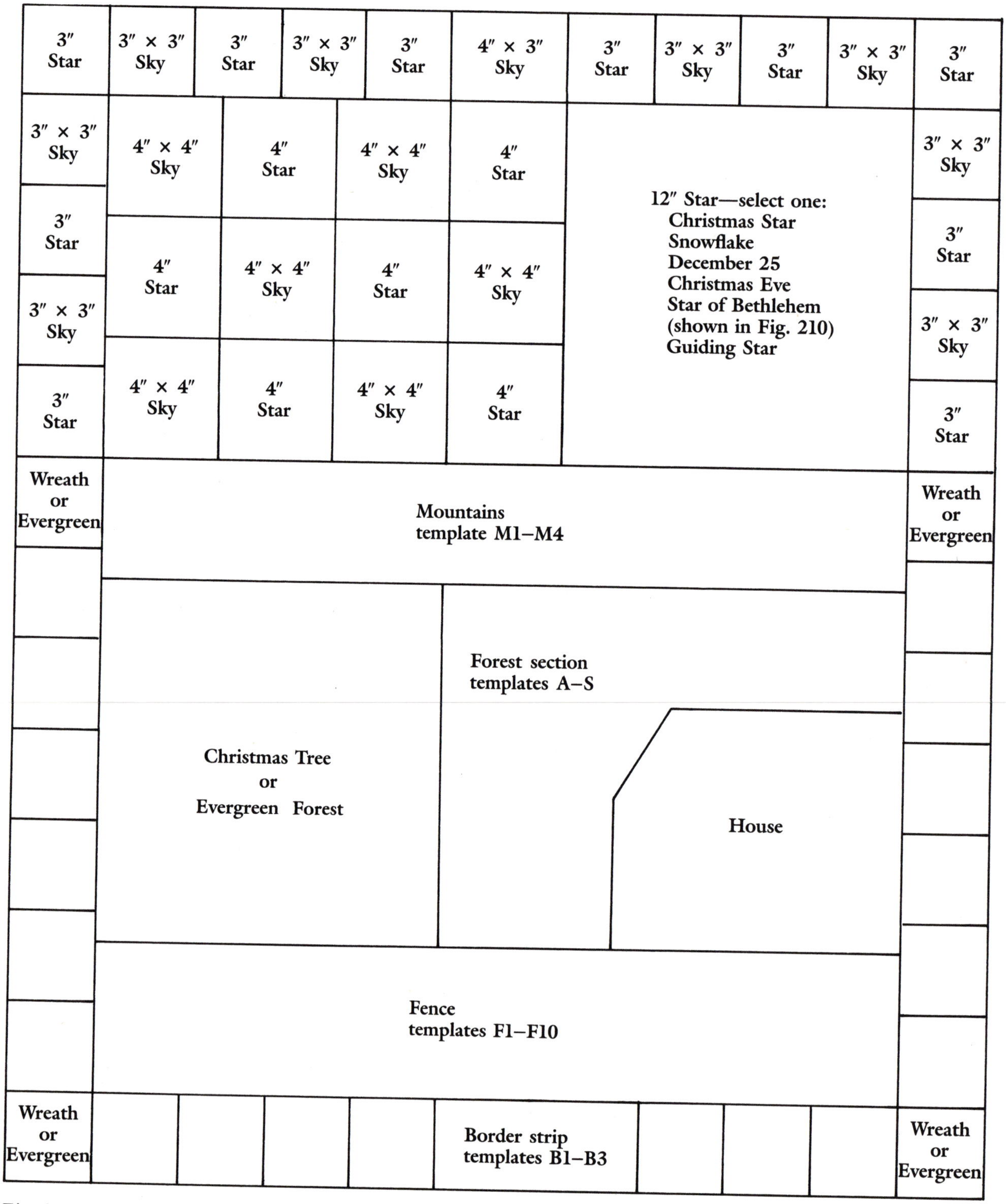

Design diagram

Top row: 3" Star | 3" × 3" Sky | 3" Star | 3" × 3" Sky | 3" Star | 4" × 3" Sky | 3" Star | 3" × 3" Sky | 3" Star | 3" × 3" Sky | 3" Star

Left column: 3" × 3" Sky | 3" Star | 3" × 3" Sky | 3" Star

Right column: 3" × 3" Sky | 3" Star | 3" × 3" Sky | 3" Star

Interior squares:
4" × 4" Sky | 4" Star | 4" × 4" Sky | 4" Star
4" Star | 4" × 4" Sky | 4" Star | 4" × 4" Sky
4" × 4" Sky | 4" Star | 4" × 4" Sky | 4" Star

12" Star—select one:
Christmas Star
Snowflake
December 25
Christmas Eve
Star of Bethlehem (shown in Fig. 210)
Guiding Star

Wreath or Evergreen

Mountains template M1–M4

Forest section templates A–S

Christmas Tree or Evergreen Forest

House

Fence templates F1–F10

Wreath or Evergreen

Border strip templates B1–B3

Fig. 212 I'll Be Home for Christmas Wall Hanging design diagram.

Fence (brown): ⅛ *yard*
Snow: ½ *yard*
House: ⅛ *yard red; scraps for door, windows, path*
Back (allows for self-binding): 1   36½" × 41½" —
1⅛ *yards**
Batting: 1   34" × 39"
Separate binding (optional): 1   1" × 150" —¼ *yard*
Sleeve for hanging (optional): 1   3" × 34"**
**The yardage for the back includes enough fabric for a*
sleeve.

Construct the wall hanging in 7 sections: study the design diagram. First, sew the sections together; then add a border.

Sky: Cut the sky background squares, following the above measurements. Select your 4-inch-square stars from those given in Tree Ornaments. Use your sky fabric for the bright fabric specified in the list of templates for each star. Piece 6 stars, as directed in the individual instructions. Arrange the stars and background squares in 4 rows with 4 squares in each row; stitch together in rows. Stitch the rows together, matching seams carefully, to complete the sky.

Large star: Select one of these designs from the preceding chapter: Christmas Eve, Christmas Star, December 25, Guiding Star, Snowflake, or Star of Bethlehem. Your chosen star will have to be adapted slightly to make it appear to "hang" in the sky. To achieve this effect, cut all the pieces surrounding the star from the sky fabric. Do the patchwork as directed in the individual instructions. Stitch the star to the right edge of the sky.

Mountains:
Easy

| M1 | 1 mountain fabric | M3 | 5 sky |
| M2 | 2 sky | M4 | 5 mountain fabric |

Sew an M2 to the left edge of M1. Sew an M3 to the top left edge of each M4; sew the diagonal strips just made to each other, as shown in the diagram. Sew the left edge of the strip to M1 and the right edge to the remaining M2. Stitch the mountains to the sky.

Christmas tree or forest: The Christmas Tree block is in the preceding chapter. Cut out as directed, except cut the B and D pieces from the fabric you have chosen for the field; sew the patchwork, following the individual instructions.

If you decide to create an evergreen forest, use the Evergreen design; see Tree Ornaments. Follow Fig. 213 and the list below to cut the pieces:

K	11 green	N	18 snow, 4 field fabric
L	18 snow, 4 field fabric		
M	11 brown	3½" × 3½" squares:
		3 snow, 2 field fabric

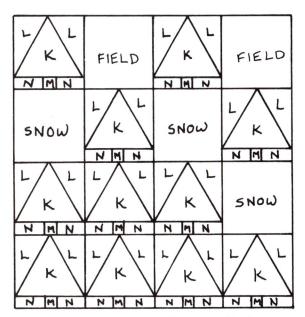

Fig. 213   Christmas tree or forest assembly diagram.

Piece each evergreen, following the individual instructions, making 9 with a snowy background and 2 with a field background. Arrange the pieced trees and the squares in 4 rows with 4 squares in each row; follow Fig. 213 or create your own arrangement, keeping the trees with the field background in the top row. Stitch the squares together in rows; then stitch the rows together, matching seams carefully, to complete the block.

House: For the templates and instructions, see House Doorstop. When cutting the roof, follow the dash lines on template A. Do the patchwork for the house, as directed in the individual instructions.

Forest section: This section includes the chimney for the house and the field behind the house.

Easy

A	1 snow	K	1 tree fabric
B	1 red (to match house)	L	1 snow
C	1 field fabric	M	1 snow
D	1 field fabric	N	2 snow
E	1 field fabric	O	1 snow
F	1 tree fabric	P	1 snow
G	1 field fabric	Q	1 tree fabric
		R	1 snow

| H | 3 brown | | S | 1 snow |
| J | 2 snow | | | |

Sew A to the top left edge of the pieced house. Sew C and D to opposite sides of B, as shown. Sew E to C-B-D. Sew G to F; then sew F to C-E. Set aside.

Next, sew a J to each side of H. Sew L and M to opposite sides of K. Sew N and O to opposite sides of one H. Sew P to N-H. Sew Q to R; then sew Q-R to P-O-K-M. Sew S and N to opposite sides of the remaining H and sew to P-Q. Sew J-H-J to the top of the patchwork rectangle just made.

Sew J-R-N to the left edge of the house. Sew F-C-B-D to the top of the piece just made to complete the house and forest section.

Sew the forest section to the tree or evergreen forest; then sew to the base of the mountains.

Fence:

Easy

F1	2 snow, 2 brown		F6	1 snow
F2	2 snow		F7	1 snow
F3	12 brown		F8	1 snow
F4	10 snow,		F9	1 snow
	10 brown		F10	1 path fabric
F5	10 snow			

Sew each snow F1 to a brown F1. Sew each brown F1 to an F2; sew an F3 to the right edge of one F1-2 and the left edge of the other.

Sew each snow F4 to a brown F4. Sew each brown F4 to an F5. Arrange the pieces just made between the F3's, as shown in the diagram; join together in 2 fence strips. Sew F6 to the top of the long fence strip and F7 to the right edge. Sew F9 to the left edge of the short fence strip; then sew F8 to the top. Sew the strips just made to each side of F10. Sew the fence strip to the bottom of the wall hanging to complete the design.

Upper border: Cut the sky background squares and rectangle following the measurements given in the Requirements. Select either the Bright Star or Shining Star design in Tree Ornaments. Use your sky fabric for the bright fabric specified in the list of templates for the star. Piece 10 stars, as directed in the individual instructions.

Arrange 6 stars and the plain squares and rectangle horizontally for the top row of the border, following the assembly diagram; stitch together. With the remaining stars and sky squares, arrange 2 vertical strips for the upper side borders with 4 pieces in each strip; stitch together.

Lower border: Select either the Evergreen or Wreath design in Tree Ornaments. Use your snow fabric for the background of each square. Piece 23 trees or wreaths as directed in the individual instructions.

For the border strip, cut these templates:

| B1 | 1 path fabric | | B3 | 1 snow |
| B2 | 1 snow | | | |

Sew B2 and B3 to opposite sides of B1. Sew 4 trees or wreaths together horizontally and join to B3. Sew 5 trees or wreaths together horizontally and join to B2.

Arrange 2 vertical strips of 7 trees or wreaths each for the lower side borders; stitch together.

Complete the side borders by sewing the upper and lower border strips together. Sew the side borders to the left and right edges of the wall hanging. Sew the stars to the top and the trees or wreaths to the bottom of the wall hanging.

Quilting: See Assembling a Project for Quilting for necessary instructions. Quilt the sky, mountains, field, trees, house and path, as shown in the assembly diagram. Use brown quilting thread for the roof of the house; outline-quilt the door and windows with white thread. Quilt the large star, following the individual instructions (if making the Star of Bethlehem, quilt as shown in the assembly diagram; then outline-quilt the central star). Outline-quilt each of the stars, the fence, and border trees or wreaths.

Finishing: Bind the wall hanging following your chosen method; see Binding a Project. Fabric has been allowed for self-binding the project; if you are adding a separate binding, trim the back so that it is even with the top; then proceed.

Hanging: Turn all raw edges of the sleeve ¼ inch to the wrong side; repeat the folding and topstitch in place. Pin the sleeve flat across the top of the wall hanging on the back, centering it between the sides; slip-stitch each long edge of the sleeve securely to the wall hanging.

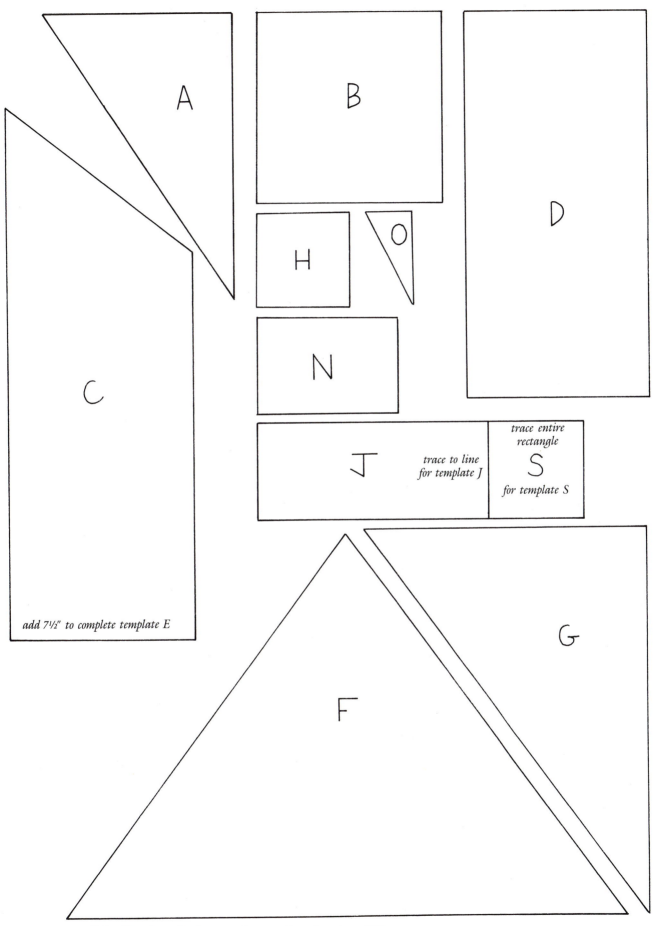

A

B

D

O

H

C

N

J

*trace to line
for template J*

*trace entire
rectangle*

S

for template S

add 7½" to complete template E

G

F

Fig. 214   *Templates for forest section;* *continued on page 138.*

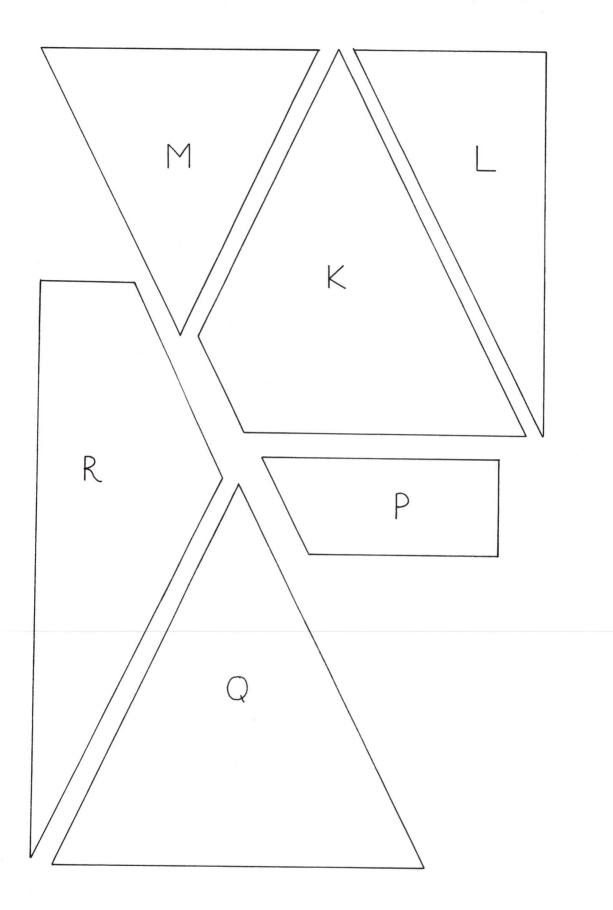

(Fig. 214 continued.)

138

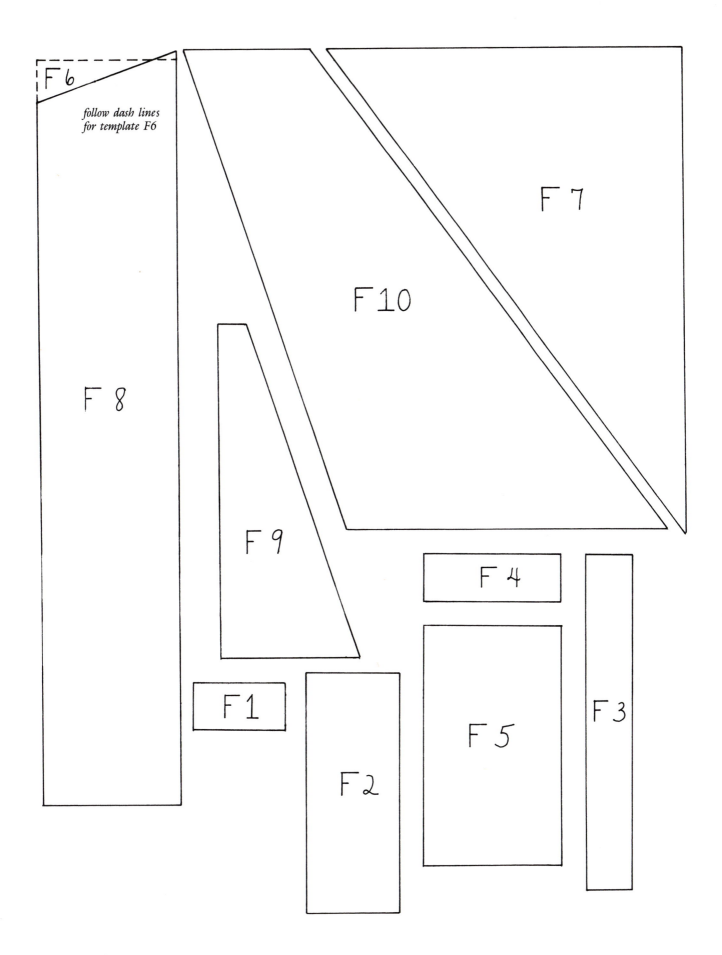

F 6

*follow dash lines
for template F6*

F 7

F 10

F 8

F 9

F 4

F 3

F 1

F 5

F 2

Fig. 215 *Templates for fence section.*

139

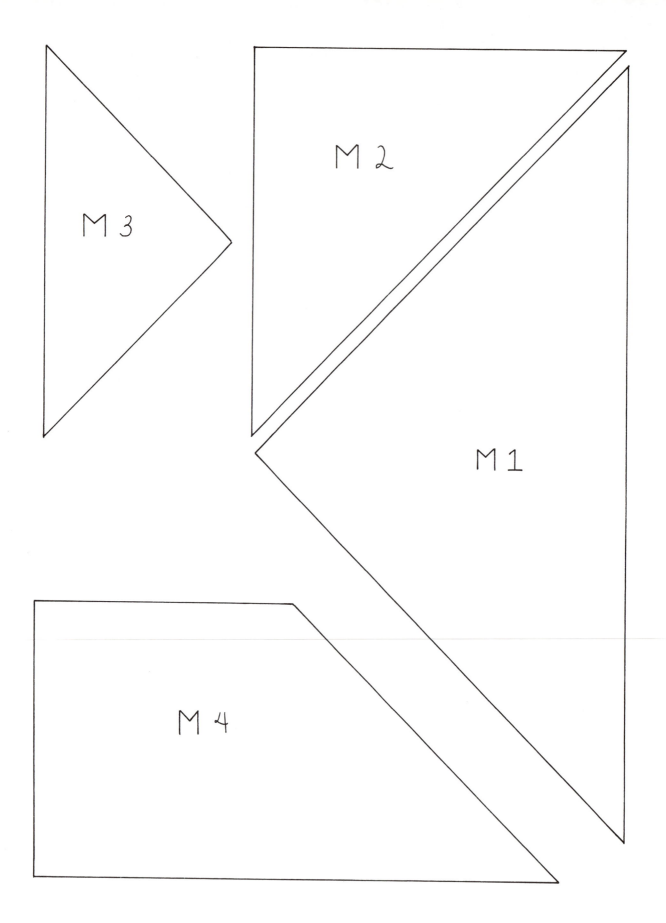

Fig. 216   Templates for mountains.

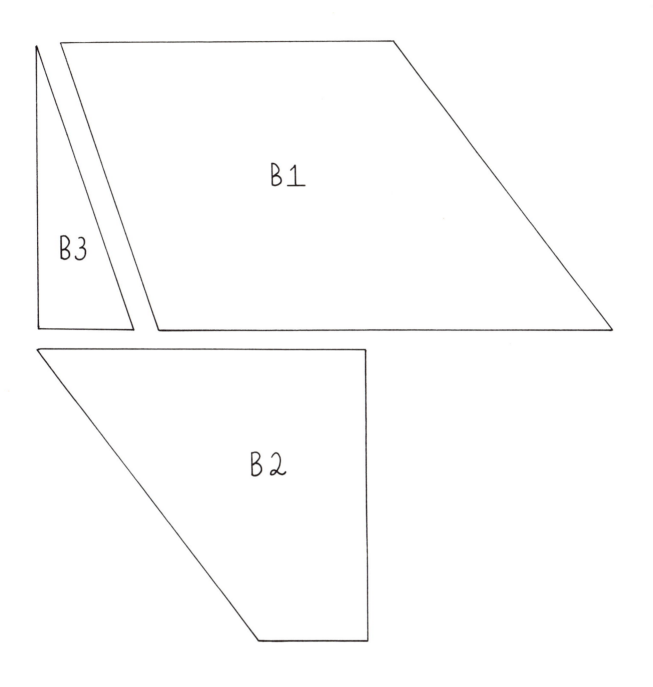

Fig. 217   Templates for border strip.

Index

ABOUT THE AUTHOR

Linda Seward, author of *Patchwork Quilts for Kids You Love* (Sterling Publishing Co., Inc., 1985), is an active needleworker and designer. She graduated from Tobe-Coburn School for Fashion Careers and has a B.S. degree in home economics from Douglass College, Rutgers University. Many of her designs have been published in needlework magazines and, during her career, she has edited many needlework and crafts books. Linda now lives in London with her husband. Besides writing, she continues to explore new ideas for needlework by creating her own captivating projects and is at work on her upcoming patchwork book.